Praise for
Liturgies for Wholeness

"In the throes of a trial, words can fail us. And in the mundanity of simple routines, we can forget their importance. *Liturgies for Wholeness* is a lifeline for those praying in the day-to-day and the turbulent. Elledge and Moore generously share their poetic prayers, which have helped me pause, reflect, and praise. I'm keeping my copy close."

—LAUREN WINDLE, public speaker and
author of *Notes On Love* and *Notes On Feminism*

"We live in a time where the secular-sacred divide has been rightly problematized. This book is one very important contribution to curing the sickly dualism at the heart of our culture, which sees the body and spirit, mind and heart, and the sacred and secular as distinct, unconnected realities. In *Liturgies for Wholeness,* the healing power of tearing down such a harmful divide has formed these everyday liturgies that reveal the extraordinary miracle of each ordinary moment. This book is a must-have for deepening one's contemplative attention of God by bringing prayerful integration to these nefarious dualisms that wrongfully control our lives and culture."

—Dr. David Bennett, Oxford academic,
theologian, and author of *A War of Loves*

"I was a massive fan of *Liturgies for Hope,* and *Liturgies for Wholeness* is the perfect companion to it! Often I find myself searching for the words that bring language to what I'm experiencing but are also laced with the hope and truth of Scripture. Elledge and Moore have once again managed to marry both of those in the most beautiful way! This book has enhanced my prayer life in so many ways, and I have already bought copies for everyone I know. Become good friends with the table of contents so you can find a liturgy for the exact moment you need it or for when you want to send encouragement to someone else."

—Meghan Ryan Asbury, author of *You Are Not Behind*

"*Liturgies for Wholeness* takes the aches of my heart, pins them to grace, and spirals them back out with love to the world. Prayer is meant to be earthed in the ordinary, and the unexpected invitation to prayer—in my imperfections, my hours, my naps, and my haircuts—expands my language and longings. Make this book your companion in the daily journey toward wholeness in the presence of God."

—Sarah Yardley, author of *More > Change*
and mission lead of Creation Fest UK

"Elledge and Moore have done it again. They have waded into the waters of our shared experiences and said the unsayable. They have named the shadows and the light, and they have given us words, in such rich and poetic fashion, for when we don't have them. This book has become a staple in our home, a voice of reassurance and a much needed reminder of the hope we have. Bravo, my friends!"

—Joshua Luke Smith, performing artist, pastor, and author

Liturgies for Wholeness

Liturgies
for Wholeness

60 Prayers to Encounter the Depth,
Creativity, and Friendship of God
in Ordinary Moments

AUDREY ELLEDGE
AND ELIZABETH MOORE

WATERBROOK

Published in the United States by WaterBrook,
an imprint of Random House, a division of
Penguin Random House LLC.

WaterBrook and colophon are registered trademarks
of Penguin Random House LLC.

Hardback ISBN 978-0-593-44282-1
Ebook ISBN 978-0-593-44283-8

The Cataloging-in-Publication Data is on file with the Library of Congress

Printed in the United States of America on acid-free paper

waterbrookmultnomah.com

2 4 6 8 9 7 5 3 1

First Edition

Book design by Elizabeth A. D. Eno

Most WaterBrook books are available at special
quantity discounts for bulk purchase for premiums,
fundraising, and corporate and educational needs
by organizations, churches, and businesses.
Special books or book excerpts also can be created
to fit specific needs. For details, contact
specialmarketscms@penguinrandomhouse.com.

For our mothers, who carry us in prayer

Contents

CONTENTS

CONTENTS

CONTENTS

A Note on Liturgy

Perhaps *liturgy* is a new word for you. Maybe you grew up in a tradition that practiced liturgy, but it feels irrelevant and outdated now. Or maybe liturgy, with its rootedness and sacraments, is something you have only recently longed for.

Historically, liturgical prayer refers to responsive, communal prayer that is usually repeated in a worship service to direct people toward God. By repeating words based on Scripture—which has been spoken by all sorts of people throughout history—liturgical prayer invites us into rich communion with both God and generations of worshippers who came before us. Liturgy reminds us that we are not alone—our stories are woven together with the stories of others who have repeated the same words and who have reached for God in their pain and joy.

Formation is at the heart of liturgy. Through liturgy, we learn the practices and rhythms of faith that shape our hearts, minds, desires, convictions, and whole selves. Liturgy forms us in the way of Jesus, which is to say, it forms us into the people we are meant to be.

In this book, when we use the word *liturgy,* we are referring to an original, pre-written prayer based on the comfort, truth, and wonder found in Scripture. We believe our daily lives present us with an opportunity to participate in liturgy, so we put words to some common experiences—washing our face, grocery shopping, napping, dancing—all through which we can encounter the Divine. You'll also find prayers to guide you through life's highs and lows: falling in love, healing a broken heart, receiving a diagnosis, overthinking, forgiving.

If you're at a loss for words, need fresh inspiration, or just feel exhausted, we pray these liturgies provide a steady, comforting framework for your own prayers. We wrote these liturgies to give language to the wonder and wrestling in your mind, body, heart, and soul. And we hope these liturgies invite you into a community of people praying the same words, anchored in the knowledge that God sees us and calls us beloved.

How to Use This Book

We are all beginners when it comes to prayer.

If you've never prayed a day in your life, you are welcome here. If prayer is a part of your daily spiritual practice, you are welcome here. If you've picked up this book seeking nourishment through prayer—welcome. In these pages, you'll find liturgies to orient your entire being toward wholeness. By addressing topics that pertain to the mind, the senses, the body, the heart, and the soul, as well as our homes, communities, and world, these prayers aim to bring all the parts of ourselves to God.

This book will live best on your nightstand, in your backpack, or on the passenger seat of your car—available to be picked up as needed. While you could read this book cover to cover, we hope you frequently scan the table of contents and find language that speaks to what you, a friend, or a loved one is going through. Feel free to use these liturgies individually, in the quiet of your room or in the chaos of your life, as well as corporately, reciting them as a community with the intention of being collectively formed.

As you read one liturgy at a time, take a deep breath. Read each line slowly and thoughtfully. Allow every word to land softly on your heart. Speak them directly to God and resolve to be fully honest with Him. Hope more wildly than you've ever dared to before and listen quietly for the Father's encouraging response.

At the end of each liturgy, you'll find Scripture references that inspired these prayers. We encourage you to spend additional time with these verses on your own and ask what the Holy Spirit may be speaking to you through His Word. And as you engage in ongoing conversation with God, may your prayers transcend words, leading you into constant communion with your Maker and continual nearness to His presence.

Above all, as you read and pray, may God remind you that He is kind, gracious, beautiful, and good. May you sense, deep in your soul, that He longs to hear from you, no matter how fractured you may feel. If the pursuit of wholeness begins with brokenness, then may we come to the feet of Jesus together, free and open with our imperfections, examining what needs repair and looking beyond ourselves to the only One who can make us whole.

For the Mind

COME, LET US BEGIN with the mind, stubborn yet elastic, forceful yet so easily led. As we listen for the quiet voice of truth, let us emerge from the hollow of our inflated egos and linger in the light. Though we may need to unlearn to understand, we take heart, for curiosity is a wonderful place to begin. Let us come to our questions with courage, for they are the seedbed of renewal. Let us explore the vast unknown of our minds together, for though we are often lost, we are not alone. May our imaginations stretch beyond themselves, for the Spirit awaits at the edge of the world's wisdom. May our thoughts fly upward until they are weightless with clarity and far from the Liar's reach. May we resist deceit and ponder goodness until our bodies and souls follow suit, until our homes and neighborhoods and world are restored. May we give and receive grace in generous doses, for the journey to wholeness will take time and creativity and a multitude of mistakes, but the work will surely be completed. We are led by a faithful Guide.

A Liturgy for Those Who Think They Are Always Right

Here I am, Lord,
Your strong-willed child,
Your passionate apprentice,
ready and willing to ride into battle
with my armor on and my shield up.

This boldness of heart is a gift—
worthy of gratitude and cultivation.
Yet an urgency for accuracy
and a devotion to discovering the right way
have taught me to rely on my mind,
overvaluing the power of knowledge
and undervaluing the power of listening,
defending not only what is good,
but also myself and my heart,
which is far more tender than I realize.

And so, wise and gentle Teacher,
relieve me of my armor—
these tools of self-protection—
and help me be a humble student,
that I may comprehend what is beyond my understanding.

I cannot change my nature,
but I can wrestle it closer to You.
Bend me
like malleable clay,
like heated metal,
to be more like You.

You, who possess the strength of kings.
You, who restrain this power for good.
You, who discern when to hold fast and when to
      relent.

Here is my heart, Lord—
fierce yet soft—
may it be trained and restrained
by the counsel of Your Spirit.
Show me the shape my strength should take,
and place Your hands over mine
as we form, together, a heart that imitates Yours.

Open my eyes to all I do not know.
Open my mind to the wonder of learning.
Open my mouth so that I may speak with measured
      wisdom.

For every thought, I need You.
For every decision, I need You.
For every impulse, I need You.

My ability to be right is not what pleases You,
nor what secures my respect from others.
Rather my ability to trust You,
to listen to You,
to walk in step with Your Spirit—
this is what anchors my thoughts.

Amen.

Psalm 16 • Matthew 11:29 • John 5:19–22 • 2 Corinthians 10:3–5, 17–18 • Ephesians 4:29 • Philippians 2:1–11 • James 3:13–17

A Liturgy for Those Who Think They Are Always Wrong

Oh Lord, my insufficiencies roar loudly in my ear,
and the threatening voice of fear silences me.

With the weight of self-doubt dragging behind me,
I come to You.

With the belief that others will always know better than me,
I come to You.

With eyes that regard myself as small and limited,
I come to You.

Belittled by grand arguments, I ask,
Do You see me?

Ashamed of my wrong answers, I wonder,
Do You see me?

Afraid of what I do not know, I whisper,
Do You see me?

With a disproportionate amount of distrust
in my own understanding,
I have claimed ignorance as an identity,
constantly assuming incorrectness
rather than honoring the cognitive abilities You have
        given me.
But You have destined me for more than second-
        guessing.

Thank You, Lord, that You do not condemn me,
that my fear and timidity are not hidden from You.
Thank You, Lord, that You move toward me with
        compassion,
though I feel I have done nothing of significance
        for You.

I lay before You now the imperfect and lovely gift of
        my mind,
this profound miracle of thinking,
this image-bearing ability to reason.

Let me love You, oh Lord my God,
by believing in the potential You have created.

Let me love You by learning,
by speaking what is on my mind,
by trusting in Your wisdom,
which is accessible to all who ask.

7

Oh Lord, it is true:

without the clarifying light of Your Spirit,

my mind is prone to darkness,

seeing dimly the truth You have established.

But You have tucked the mystery of wisdom

into the body and blood of Christ.

May I not deny the potency of this mind You have

given me

but with it seek out the hidden wonders of Your world.

May I not boast in my ignorance,

nor in my intelligence,

but in Your life and resurrection,

Your love and grace,

Your mercy and kindness.

Amen.

Psalm 103:13 • Proverbs 3:5–6 • Matthew 22:37 • 1 Corinthians 1:18–31; 2:6–16 •
2 Timothy 1:7 • James 1:5

A Liturgy for Cultivating Imagination

Oh God of artistry and ingenuity,
inspiration and invention,
creation and enterprise.

Yours is the Great Imagination—
forming entire worlds and galaxies
out of the overflow of Your creativity.
You make the clouds Your chariot.
You ride on the wings of the wind.
You formed the Leviathan to play in the sea.
You even created us, our earth, and the infinity that
    surrounds us.

You have instilled imagination deeply within us,
designing us to create with our minds and our spirits.
We are imprinted with this aspect of Your image
and desire to be good stewards of such a marvelous gift.

9

Through imagination,
may we better comprehend
this world that You have made.
May we perceive beauty beyond reason
and explore the eternity You have set in our hearts.
May we be astonished
with hope for the future of the world,
until our idols appear as small and powerless as they
        really are.

Enrich our intelligence for the renewal of the earth
and send forth Your Spirit into our minds,
for without Your breath—the source of true life—
we can produce only lifeless things.

Let us not depend on conventional or cultural wisdom,
but as we listen for the stirring of Your voice,
may Your holy imagination enlighten our thoughts.

As we wait for You, oh Creative One,
fuel us with divine inspiration.
May stunning canvases be painted.
May transcendent symphonies be scored.
May tales that are written for children bring grown men
        to their knees.

Receive our ideas and our crafts,
our sculptures and our songs,
as offerings of praise,
as sweet-smelling incense—

filling Your throne room
with the aroma of unhindered inspiration.

Amen.

Genesis 1:1, 27, 31 • Psalm 27:4; 104; 135:13–18 • Proverbs 3:19 • Ecclesiastes 3:11–13 • Isaiah 40:26; 65:17–18 • John 14:16–17, 25–26; 15:4 • Ephesians 5:1

A Liturgy for Overthinking

Oh God who speaks calm into chaos,
who orders disorder,
who rules over unruliness—
my mind is caught in a spiral,
utterly lost to the anarchy of intrusive thoughts.

I have played out every possible scenario in my head,
running through the what-ifs and how-comes,
believing if I think long or hard enough,
I will somehow bring myself clarity.

I have tried and failed to steady myself with solutions,
to shelter myself with willpower,
seeking asylum in logical theories,
only for the tantalizing promise of security to vanish
    like smoke.

But all of this thinking has left me lost at sea
and no closer to meaningful answers.
My thoughts have spread themselves thin,
and I hardly have any strength left.

So I bring my exhausted mind to You
and invite You into this space of confusion.

When my thoughts wander,
redirect them to Your steadying presence.
When my mind sets off on a path leading nowhere,
guide me back to Your side.
When I cannot be still,
soothe the turbulence within me
the same way You calmed the wind and waves.

May I entrust all I do not know
and all I cannot grasp to You.
Help me comprehend what is meant for me in due time.

As I place my absolute faith in You,
may I be met by my whole self,
made full and complete in Christ—
not boasting in my own understanding
but surrendered in humble confidence
to the One who fathoms all that I cannot.

Amen.

Joshua 1:9 • Psalm 24; 46:10; 85:8 • Proverbs 3:5–6 • Isaiah 26:3

A Liturgy for Before
a Performance

Oh Lord, I confess to taking myself too seriously,
to believing the world will stop turning if I perform with
anything less than perfection.
The praise of people lures me in,
and I indulge in fantasies of accolades and admiration.
Guard me, oh God, against this poison of pride.

These fluttering butterflies are neither signs of my
       impending doom nor success
but rather reminders of my ability to care,
of my enjoyment of this task You have graciously given.

Oh Emmanuel, transform my fizzing nerves into
       playfulness,
into a childlike focus on the process and not the finish line.
May peace cover my voice, my hands, my feet, my mind.
May self-consciousness yield to self-giving

as I steward the gifts You have given me for the good
        of the world.
May even the stage become a place
on which I can secretly savor Your company,
Your ever-present help and joy.

Grant me the proper portion of preparation,
while leaving room for Your Spirit to move.
Help me perform as a complete person,
as my whole self,
for I have already been given fullness in You.

Now I rest in Your freedom, oh Lord.
I indulge in the fearlessness and boldness I cannot create
        on my own,
and yet I can always access.

May the spotlight turn dim in comparison to the radiance
        that comes from You.
May I care less about approval than courage.
And above all, oh Holy One, may Your applause and
        pleasure
be my sweetest and sole reward.

Amen.

Psalm 32:7; 34:5; 46:1 • Luke 12:12 • 1 Corinthians 4:5 • Galatians 1:10 • Ephesians 3:19 • Colossians 3:23

A Liturgy for Right After
a Panic Attack

Oh God who sees me,
be not far off.
Oh God who is witness to the hurricane of my mind,
do not delay.

I cannot name what has overtaken me,
but I can describe it:
the shadows overwhelming,
the fear screaming,
the lies shooting through my defenses like arrows.

I feel like an outsider to my own body,
trapped and disoriented,
aware of my unrelenting fragility.

Breath of Life, come into these lungs.
Clutching onto You,

16

I admit I fear the next wave,
worried I could lose myself—
getting tossed to sea and shattered.

Oh God, where else could I go?

My head feels like a grave, buried and dark.
But death is not a sentence I have to accept,
because of You, oh Christ.

You are the God who became human
in the lowest and loneliest circumstances,
in a place where the light was dimming.
You are the conqueror of pits,
of places where the shadows loom.

Oh Jesus, in Your light, make these fears look small.
Turn panic into ancient history.
May this experience with anxiety tether me to You
and keep me in step with softness.
Widen my compassion for those familiar with this pain.

I miss the days before I knew this terror.
Right now, I don't feel at home in this body,
in this broken mind,
but I long to be whole with You.
I ache to become what I believe.

Breathing Exercise

Breathe in, and as you exhale, repeat each line:

I believe You see me.

I believe that my despair will be redeemed.

I believe that I am not damaged.

I believe that You have the final word.

I believe that peace is found in You.

I believe that love is the opposite of fear.

I believe that where my strength fails, Yours is
         proven better.

I believe You reach into the pit and pull me out.

I believe, before that, You sit in the pit with me.

I believe this will not last forever.

I believe I will feel joy again.

Amen.

Genesis 16:13 • Psalm 22; 30:11–12; 40:1–3; 70:5; 107:27–30 • John 6:68 • 1 Corinthians 15:55 • 2 Corinthians 1:4 • Philippians 4:7

A Liturgy for Rising
Above a Mistake

Gracious God, please redeem what I have done.

I am stuck in the mercilessness of my own mind,
replaying the moment in which I harmed.
Dwelling in this memory of pain
and brooding with regret,
I need You to pull me from this pit.

In my faltering efforts to be good, I have still made a mess.
 I have hurt with reckless words.
 I have forgotten a promise.
 I have neglected patience.
 I have failed people I love.

And yet, to this I still cling: You will mend what
 is shattered,
weave together what I unspooled,

and wash clean the smudges of my blunders.
It is Your delight to do the impossible,
to paint new mercies every morning.
It is Your cross, Jesus, that covers my mistakes.

Oh Healer, give me the courage to own what I have done
and the bravery to move on.
Startle me with grace,
with how You fling my transgression to the far side
      of the sea.
It is not the past in which I should live,
so show me what I can glean from this lesson to carry in
      the future
and what useless baggage I can discard in the unblemished
      present.

Protect, oh Lover, the people I have hurt.
Tend to their wounds in ways I cannot.
Though I do not deserve Your work on my behalf,
restore what was broken by my folly.

Oh God, repairer of all things,
You do not condemn my weakness.
Oh Jesus, great cleanser of my sins,
You are the eternal, glorious proof that my mistakes are
      not held against me.

Amen.

Psalm 40:1–3; 51:7; 103:1–4, 11–14 • Isaiah 1:18 • 1 John 1:9

A Blessing for Imperfection

If you fear that you are not enough
    or that you do not have what it takes,
if you fear that all you have built will be lost
    or that what you have is worthless,
if you find yourself rehearsing
    all of the ways you could fail—
may you see yourself as God sees you:
    secure and accepted,
    resting on the foundation of *His* perfection.

Oh child, may you fall swiftly
into the freedom of knowing
that you are not the sum of the things you got right.

May all your imperfect pieces
come together in Christ
and make you whole.

May you cling to your Creator's grace
and exist in the uniqueness of you:
the object of His delight,
the source of His pleasure.

May failure not be an end to be feared
but an invitation to draw closer
to the One who has taken your lack
and filled it with life—
the One who will never despise
your tender, needy heart.

May you know a Father who does not fail,
and may His constancy liberate you
to be all that you are.
May you gaze upon His goodness,
and discover new beauty blooming within you.

By faith and the power of God,
may you know that it is okay
to exist in imperfection—
for through this surrender
you are disarming the dominion of fear
and taking up the authority of Perfect Love.

Amen.

Psalm 27:4; 51:10–17 • Zephaniah 3:17 • 2 Corinthians 12:9–10 • Ephesians 2:4–5 •
Colossians 3:3 • 1 John 4:18

For the Senses

ALLOW YOUR SENSES TO tell you that you are in the world, that you are a part of it. Let creation speak through touch. Let it sing through taste. Let it nuzzle up close to you with its wet nose, as if to say: *I am alive and you are too.* Consider the pleasant pressure of your thumbnail as it slips under the skin of an orange—how oil and zest burst forth, how for a moment you are caught up in a bloom of citrus. Notice how a sunbaked leather seat, a bouquet of lilies, or a distant train whistle can instantly trigger a memory. How a sunset arrests your full attention. You are experiencing the world and all of its dimensions, sifting through the surface as well as what's underneath. How curious that you have not yet run out of things to explore, how these tangible delights unlock something inside of you, how your senses become portals into an invisible reality.

So sink your body into this experience of the earth. Take in more than you think you can. Be grounded and tactile. Allow sight, smell, and sound to be your pathfinders. Let taste and touch connect you to the unseen world. For every sensory experience is a clue to something greater, a part of something whole. Though the resolution may feel far off, like a melody that has drifted away too soon, this is how it begins—the prelude to the song we will sing the rest of our days.

A Liturgy for the Morning

God of endless beginnings,
today is a blank canvas
for You to create something new.

As early light slips in through the window
and my scent drifts up from the pillowcase,
I open my eyes and ears
to all that surrounds me:
the newborn sunlight kissing my nose,
the faint breeze sighing against my skin—
all of it announcing the arrival of daybreak
and illuminating the miracle of Your faithfulness,
for You conceived of mornings in the beginning
and artfully craft the sunrise day after day.

As I start this new day, I remember
Your love—loyal and constant—

and Your mercies that never come to an end.
They are reestablished every morning.
Great is Your care for us.

I come to You exactly as I am today,
for You love to hear my voice.

You are not surprised by my worries and doubts.
You are not disappointed in my humanity.
You invite me to share the full weight of who I am with You:
my joy and my sadness,
my loneliness and my grief.
For You know my feelings from afar
and perceive my thoughts before I do.
I begin this day with an honest exhale,
knowing I do not shoulder my burdens alone.

As I listen to the even cadence of my breath,
I release my worries to You,
for You provide my daily bread—I lack nothing.
Quiet my inner being and allow me to be still.
Transport me to our secret place
where I sense Your nearness,
where I am held firmly but gently in Your arms.

This morning, and every morning,
may I be thrilled to remember
that You are making all things new.

As the day hastens forward,
may I remain aware of Your sacred presence.

And when I temporarily forget You,

may the distance to reconnection be short.

May I know the way to our place of peaceful communion,

and may You become easier to find with each passing day.

Amen.

Job 38:4–7 • Psalm 5:3; 23:1–3 • Ecclesiastes 11:6 • Lamentations 3:21–26 • John 1:1–5 • Revelation 21:5; 22:16

A Liturgy for Browsing
a Museum

Come, oh Lord,
into this treasury
of restoration and recollection.

Come, walk these halls—
breathe upon these memories,
these monuments,
these masterpieces.
Take us by the hand,
and show us how You remember.

Move with us, as we explore each room.
Guide our eyes with intuition and curiosity,
as You reveal to us the imperishable wisdom
You have written upon these walls.

Thank You that human expression transcends
        language,
that our longing for *more* echoes throughout generations.
Thank You for these intimate glimpses into the past
and the tangible remnants of those who have gone
        before us.

As we look upon these artifacts and elements,
may we celebrate what has brought us beauty
and mourn what has brought us pain.

As we study customs and cultures that are not
        our own,
may we ponder what we do not understand
and learn from the facets of the unfamiliar.

As we witness—collectively and individually—
these sacred snatches of humanity,
may we be inquisitive stewards,
mindful of our bodies
as we move through galleries at just the right pace,
honoring each exhibit with our time and attention.

As we behold beauty and mystery together,
may we pause to linger over pieces that take our
        breath away—
even if we do not know why—
for perceiving glory without fully understanding it
is one of the marvelous ways You draw us to Yourself.

May entire compositions and single brushstrokes
        enthrall us.
May the playfulness of color and the tactility of texture
        astonish us.
May awe come upon us as we remember You, our Maker,
and the simple, powerful word by which You created
the heavens and the earth and all that is in them.

Antiquity and artistry are Yours,
and surely You are present in everything that has
        been made.

May we see glimpses of Your glory from the past.
May musky smells remind us of Your presence through
        the ages.
May we touch what Your image-bearers touched,
and experience Your presence close to our fingertips.

May the conservation and preservation of former years
reveal more of who You are and who You have always
        been.

May this museum be a sanctuary for Your glory.

Amen.

Genesis 1:27 • Psalm 27:4; 65:8; 96:6; 104:24 • Acts 2:43 • Colossians 1:16 • Hebrews 11:3

A Liturgy for Unplugging

Oh Jesus, You are our model for retreating,
for taking time away from noise to pray.
Show me how stillness is not just a luxury
but rather a discipline,
an obedience.

When muscle memory has me reaching first for my phone,
when I've drunk too deeply of news,
when I've scrolled mindlessly and the world crowds
        my thoughts,
Oh Lord, empty my hands
and help me to unplug.

I am weary of knowing too much
and taxed by the constancy of idle chatter.
I long to join a different sort of dialogue,

to disconnect from what does not nourish or benefit
       my soul,
and to reconnect with what is right and true.

What a strange time we live in,
when isolation and constant availability co-exist,
when curiosity can be satisfied with a click.

Oh Creator, this is what I know is true:
no screen can compare to the sun,
no device can compete with the lilies of the field,
no notifications can replace flesh and blood,
and no headline can compete with Your voice.

How can we be tethered to something so small
when the whole of creation looms ready for us?
If I do not look up and worship,
then surely the trees will clap their hands
and the stones will cry out in chorus.
Oh Christ, I do not want to miss this.

Ground your feet, pause, breathe, and move slowly through
these words:

Grant me the grace to sit in discomfort,
in silence,
to embrace boredom and see where it leads,
creating room to hear what You might want to say.
Lift my chin to see the people around me,
to be content with questions
instead of instantaneous answers.

Free my mind and body from this cycle of addiction,
and let me prize wisdom more than knowing everything.

I admit that I fear the yet-unknown needs that may arise
while I unplug,
but I trust You will always take care of what I cannot.
May I understand I am free to log on and free to log off
and can rely on You to determine which is best.

Amen.

Exodus 33:14 • Psalm 46:10 • Isaiah 55:12 • Matthew 6:25–34; 11:28–30 •
Mark 1:35–36; 2:27; 6:32 • Luke 19:40 • John 16:33 • Philippians 4:8

A Liturgy for
Paying Attention

Oh Christ who lingered,
who listened,
who welcomed interruption,
let us be generous with attention.

Busyness tricks us into scarcity,
into clutching on to time as if we could lose it.
Distracted by yesterday's failures and tomorrow's fears,
we forget the gift of today.
We long to stand attentive,
to be startled by creation again,
to be astounded by what has faded to familiarity.

May we take notice of the lives we have been given.
May we tune our ears when a friend speaks,
make eye contact with strangers,
touch fields of flowers,

become students of trees.
May we regard how even dishes and dust have something
        to teach.
May our focus be always on You, looking for Your finger-
        prints in the world,
for to stay curious is to stay present.

May awe be the filter through which we experience
        the ordinary.

Lay claim to our lives again so we can
attend fully to this moment.
Slow our pace and settle our spirits
so we may bear witness to beauty,
to details in the myriad stories around us.

May our attention feel more like a prayer that never ceases,
like a rope that tethers us to You.
We lay down our need to perform and produce,
and choose to dawdle in nature,
to lengthen conversations,
to linger with neighbors,
to stroll instead of sprint,
to believe time is oil we can pour out on You.

Amen.

Psalm 16:8; 27:4 • Isaiah 43:19 • Matthew 6:28 • 1 Thessalonians 5:16–18 • James 1:19

A Liturgy for Napping

Oh God, I thank You for the gift of closed eyes.

When my body cries out for rest,
I praise You for this chance to recover.

When there is still much to do,
yet I cannot keep these eyes open,
I praise You for this time to pause.

When the world is "too much with me,"
I praise You for this gift of respite.

Just as You slept in the storm, oh Jesus, so can I.

Because You do not grow weary,
I am free to lie down in safety.
Thank You, kind Creator,

for this place to put my head.
Thank You, perfect Provider,
for the clarity that can come from napping,
for the muck that can melt from my mind with Your help.

Allow me the discipline to nap with moderation,
to know the difference between rest and idleness,
for I do not want to run away from my life
or hibernate when I'm called to be in the world.
Even more, help me to know true stillness.
May this nap take its proper place,
nothing more and nothing less.

Let napping remind me of my own limitations
and dependence on You.
From the beginning of creation, oh God,
You prioritized rest, so as I break from my labor,
remind me of this communion of refreshment we
        can share.
And when I awake, may what was crowding my mind
and draining my spirit
fade in comparison to Your glorious might.

Amen.

Note: This liturgy is inspired by William Wordsworth's poem "The World Is Too Much with Us."

Genesis 2:1–3 • Psalm 4:8; 121:4; 127:2 • Proverbs 3:24 • Matthew 8:23–27 • Mark 4:38–40

In Praise of Golden Hour

In this fleeting golden space between day and night,
night and day,
we remember the beauty of the in-between.

Oh God, how splendid to witness the persistence
of light,
the way it softens creation at dawn
and burns like fire at dusk
only to fade and come back—
always coming back.

Oh Creator, we so often fixate on the pitfalls of living,
with all its mess and chaos,
but golden hour reminds us of Your original intention
for goodness in this world.
As we gaze upon this miracle,
help us to long for when all will be made whole.

Oh Light of the world, the colors above are proof
of the plentiful hues and facets You hold.
Help us to study this light, for it reveals something of You.
Help us to sit in this light, for it shows us how to long
       for more.
Help us to see our whole selves in this light.
And when darkness comes, help us to embrace it too,
for shadows are backdrops for stars—
and even Eden had night.

As the sun and moon make their necessary changes,
we are reminded that transition is not the enemy
but rather an ally,
a means to depend on our Maker.
We, too, are being renewed and remade.

For now, we straddle day and night
just as we do earth and eternity:
living in one, with shining glimpses of the next.

Amen.

Job 38:4 • Psalm 18:28; 139:7–12 • John 1:5 • John 8:12 • 2 Corinthians 4:16 • Ephesians 4:22–24

A Blessing for Nightfall

As the day comes to an end,
and as Night—uncompromising—
reaches her arms into Afternoon,
may you reacquaint yourself with mystery,
with the stories told by stretching shadows.

Though she approaches like a stranger,
may Darkness give way to discovery.

Though she covers your eyes with cold hands,
may your voice call out to others in the silence.

Though you find the way lonely,
may you be curiously comforted by benevolent whispers.

Though the path may seem treacherous,
may you confront the right enemies and take the right risks.

Though you brush against Death,
may you know that what threatens in the dark is powerless
in the light.

Though unknowns settle heavy on your chest,
may the mysterious anti-gravity of darkness
relieve you of your burden.

Though you must be so tired,
may you be carried until Morning.

Though the language is unfamiliar,
may even this brief absence of light
have lovely things to say.

Oh long stretch of darkness,
of nightfall,
of cease:
we are listening.

Amen.

1 Kings 19:11–13 • Psalm 23:4; 119:105 • Matthew 7:7–8; 11:28–30 • 1 Corinthians 1:27; 2 • Hebrews 10:24–25

For the Body

WHAT DOES IT MEAN to inhabit a body? What binds your soul to this frame? What do skin and sinew have to say? The body, even in its concreteness, often leaves us with more questions than answers. We do not understand how some bodies break and never heal. We do not know why youth is so fleeting. We cannot comprehend the mystery of sleep, the profundity of cutting our hair.

But this we believe: our bodies were given to us. These muscles and nerves, sunspots and scars, are evidence of how little control we have. Yet we can tell stories through lips. Our feet carry us to friends. Our hands serve food to the hungry. Our knees hold us as we kneel to pray. Everything that matters to the spirit finds movement in our frame.

Pursue wholeness in your body. Dance. Breathe deeply. Hold your hands up to the sun. Lean against a tree, float in water. Remember your body belongs in creation. God's works are wonderful, you included. Use your body for good. Hands, tongue, eyes—all are given to you as instruments for love. Though your body may feel like a crumbling temple, remember every wrinkle, every freckle, every bone, and every inch of skin will one day be renewed.

A Liturgy for Aging

We worship You, oh Ageless One,
for though You are unbound by hours or years,
You are present with us on this tour through time.

Oh Lord,
we release control
as we follow You into the odyssey of aging,
for it is a path we cannot foresee
and an inheritance we cannot renounce.

Though we are afraid of what we do not understand,
of this pilgrimage that will take us deeper
into the secrets of humanity,
You are the Alpha and the Omega—
with us before our memories began
and with us when we take our last breath.

With each passing day,
we become slightly different creatures,
growing into and out of ourselves,
maturing into the masterpieces
You designed before we were born.

May this journey not frighten us
but fill us with wonder
as we step deeper into our eternal destinies.

Thank You for the accumulation of years,
for they have amassed a wealth of hard-won wisdom.
Thank You for all You will show us in the days to come,
for every step forward draws us closer to Your heart.

As we age, may we outgrow the immaturity of being as
        we ought
and simply be as we are,
partnering with You in honesty.

As we age, may we be relentless in our quest for
        discernment
and never cease asking You for insights
into the things we do not understand.

As we age, may we uncover the cracks in our soul
and with persistence and a gritty faith
build a firm foundation upon You.

As we age, may we grow accustomed to wrestling
        with You,

unafraid to throw our whole selves upon You,
even if it means limping with dependency,
with the freedom found in weakness.

May aging become an emergence into our truest selves,
as we flourish into a glory that transcends physicality.
May we center our life's purpose not on what can be seen
but on the unseen mysteries of eternity.

Amen.

Psalm 31:14–15; 39:4–7 • Ecclesiastes 7:10 • Isaiah 40:8 • 2 Corinthians 4:16–18 •
Revelation 22:13

A Liturgy for Loving
Your Body

Oh Creator of my body,
Steward of my soul,

My vision is easily distorted by disgust,
and my eyesight can be lessened by lies.
When I am consumed by appearance,
I am unable to rightly perceive who I truly am.
I have lived in this prison of shortsightedness for too long,
and I would desperately like to be set free.

Jesus, You understand what it is like to have a body,
to be strong and weak all at once,
so teach me how You carried Yourself in flesh.

I cannot hide my insecurities from You,
for You have already discerned my thoughts from afar.

So let me be honest with You when I am feeling low,
for You have given me unconditional acceptance through
        Christ.

As I move throughout my day,
reveal to me practical ways to celebrate
this body You've given me
and remind me that the pursuit of a perfect image
is an unreachable horizon.

Let me not be deceived by the allure of temporary
        attractiveness,
nor by my own thoughts of dissatisfaction,
as if attaining an external ideal could satisfy my longing
        for love.
But let me be confident in whatever body I have,
regardless of how I think it looks,
for it is the work of Your hands.

Holy Father, Your beauty is far more compelling
than the image of myself that lives in my head.
One day, this body will be transformed and made whole,
but until that day, oh Lord,
draw me out of negative thought spirals
and into deeper reverence and wonder—
completely in awe of all that You are.
The imperfections of my body become small and
        unentertaining
when I delight in the riches of Your love,
and when I view myself through Your eyes.

So come, Holy Spirit, and whisper the thoughts of God
        into my heart.
Help me see beyond the shell of myself—
lovely one day and hideous the next—
and open my eyes to the reality of who I *truly* am,
overshadowed by the reality of who *You* truly are.

Amen.

Psalm 34:5; 139 • Proverbs 31:30 • 2 Corinthians 5:14–15 • Philippians 3:8–11;
3:20–4:1

A Liturgy for
Seasonal Depression

Here we are again, Lord,
descending into that darkness I dread.

It arrives like clockwork—this uninvited guest
with far too many suitcases,
determined to overstay its welcome,
emptying me of everything that keeps me alive.

I wonder if You hear.
I wonder if You care.
I wonder if I am navigating this darkness
            alone.

As I pour out the depths of my soul to You,
I remind myself of what I know,
even though it is far from what I feel.

When depression feels like an overpowering master,
You walk with me through the valley of shadows.
When I do not want to get out of bed in the morning,
You crawl into bed with me.
When I cannot move, cannot hope, cannot think past
this moment,
You hold me close until the darkness passes.

God, all I want is for You to lift this cloud,
for food to taste good,
for sleep to be sweet,
for my mind to be well.

But until the fog recedes,
as it will—for it always does—
I ask for Your presence and Your patience,
for friends who will make space for me exactly as I am,
for moments of laughter and levity
and the hope of better days to come.

May the intensity of my seasonal depression
lessen each year,
but until that day comes,
I lean against You—Man of Sorrows, God of compassion.
I lean against the community You have provided.
I lean against the small delights You will bring my way.
I lean against Your love that is closer than I know.

Amen.

Psalm 23; 34:18; 42 • Isaiah 53:3 • 2 Corinthians 3:4–5

A Liturgy for
a Diagnosis

Oh God who knit me together in my mother's womb,
I have just discovered the name of my suffering
and am struggling to welcome this newcomer into
        my life.

On one hand, this diagnosis brings relief,
finally identifying the illness my body endures.

On the other hand, this diagnosis brings
        discouragement,
as naming does not mean solving or healing.

With this complicated blend of all that I feel,
I place this diagnosis into Your hands,
for You are the One who truly sees,
truly identifies,
truly regenerates.

May I never view this diagnosis
as a punishment for things I've done wrong
but rather as an opportunity to see Your power unfurled.

When this diagnosis grips me with despair,
would You send Your agents of hope to encourage me,
and would Your presence be more powerful than fear?

When this diagnosis threatens to overwhelm me,
help me take one step at a time,
trusting that Your Spirit of patience
sustains me for the long journey of healing.

In the midst of pain and discomfort,
    I cry out to You who are well acquainted with suffering.
In the midst of physical and emotional weakness,
    I cry out to You who strengthen me with Your
        nearness.
In the midst of unknowns and unanswered questions,
    I cry out to You who comprehend all biological
        conditions.

May this body You designed to heal itself
come into perfect alignment with Your will,
and may I intimately experience the authority You hold
over my health in a whole new way.

Amen.

Joshua 1:9 • Psalm 42; 103:1–5; 139; 145:18 • Jeremiah 17:14 • John 9

A Liturgy for a
Fresh Haircut

Join me as I cut my hair, oh Lord.
Be with me as I tend to these strands You have already
numbered.

If hair is old pieces of me,
then this cutting becomes a symbol of my transformed self.
Thank You for this reminder that
the old has gone and the new has come.
Thank You that I can watch this dead hair fall
and remember how You bring life,
how You have made me whole.

As pieces tumble to the ground, oh Christ,
show me what I can leave behind as I move ahead.
Teach me how to release what I cannot keep.
Help me to shed what no longer serves You.

In the same way I receive care through scissors,
so do I benefit from Your pruning, oh Gardener.
You do not shear without meaning,
for each cut from Your hand is meant to bear fruit,
each slice is meant for my good.

Allow me the delight, oh God, to savor the end result of
this fresh creation,
to bless the hands that shaped my hair.

May these locks not be my greatest adornment,
for they are here today and gone tomorrow.
Help me to not consume myself with the mirror
but rather to rejoice in the health You give my body
and in the honor it is to steward the temple
in which You reside.

Amen.

Matthew 6:30; 10:30 • John 15:2 • 2 Corinthians 5:17 • Philippians 3:13–14 •
1 Peter 3:3–4

A Liturgy for Healing

Son of God, make this body whole.

I boldly ask for the miraculous restoration
only You can do.
I reach out, hoping to touch Your hem and be healed.

Fix my hope not on this temporary flesh
but on You alone, who have the power to sustain me,
to take away this pain.

My regular rhythms have come to a halt,
and my mind wanders to past days of health,
envying the self who took wholeness for granted.

Leaning against grace,
I trust You in this sidelined state.

Somehow, help me to boast in this weakness,
for there is something here to learn about true strength.

Join me, oh Jesus, as my nearest companion.
Fill my mouth with worship,
with prayers I can give back to You.
Humor me with Your joy, which is my strength.
Open my eyes to the people I can still serve,
especially with this enlarged empathy for the sick
          and hurt.

Humble me to receive the care of others
and to be stirred by love, even in its human imperfection.
And if I do not receive what I feel I need,
show me Your tender care
and remind me I am not forgotten by the One who sees.

I do not know when I will be completely healed,
and the ambiguity of this timeline overwhelms me.
Be kind to both my body and mind, oh Creator,
as I grapple with the weight of uncertainty.

There is not much I understand,
but to this I cling:
I was not made to be sick,
I am not doomed to be paralyzed,
and my longing for healing is a desire for eternity.

Thank You, oh Christ,
that You offer Your own self for me to hold

as I long for everlasting transformation
and eagerly anticipate this body one day made whole.

Amen.

Psalm 6:2; 41:3; 103:2–4 • Jeremiah 30:17 • Luke 5:17–26; 18:38 • 2 Corinthians 12:9–10 • Hebrews 4:16 • James 5:14–15

A Liturgy for the Loss of Pregnancy

How long, oh Lord?
How long will these tears stream without end?
How long will this pain cut me like a blade?
How long will I be haunted by loss?

What I feared most has happened:
I have a precious child, with a name—
with a soul—
whom I cannot hold.

Why, oh God?

I am in need of Your consolation
as I sit in the ruins of expectations,
in the destruction of dreams.
Our preparations for life have crumbled with this theft
        by death.

I will always wonder what my baby was like,
who You knitted them in the womb to become,
how they would have fit into our family.
Countless are those who would have loved this child,
who would have welcomed and cheered for their life.

I am weighted, oh Father, by my baby's untold story.

When I go outside, signs of life feel wrong,
as if the earth did not get the message.
How do others still laugh?
How do children still play?
How can the world keep spinning?

Desperate for answers,
I know only an empty womb.
Guard me from the belief that this nightmare
is punishment from You,
that I've done something to deserve this twisted outcome.
For I believe You weep when I weep,
that Your heart shatters, too,
and that You, more than anyone, understand a parent's loss.

Send companions to sit with me in my discomfort,
to show up even if they don't understand.
Anoint their words so they feel like a balm and not a knife.
I don't need advice;
I just need presence, oh Spirit.

Though I believe my baby, healed and whole,
is with You now,

I cannot rush this lament.
Grief does not negate hope,
so with Your help I will make room for both.

I know the due date in the future will sting,
so go before me, loving God,
to all those days I must survive.

Astonish me with how You redeem that date,
so that the calendar does not dredge up dread
but rather stirs in me the assurance of hope,
of the future reunion that awaits.

One day, when tears are wiped away,
I believe our family will be made whole again,
just as my baby already is with You.

Amen.

Psalm 13; 139 • Lamentations 3:17–24 • Isaiah 53:4 • John 9:3 • 1 Corinthians 15:55 •
Revelation 21:4

A Liturgy for Dancing

Come, joyous Father, into this sanctuary of movement.
Come, delighted Son, into this moment of release.
Come, playful Spirit, into my limbs and lungs.

Breathing in, I fill my chest with Your lightness.
Breathing out, I release myself of all that is not grace.

As I begin to move, I surrender to the thrill
of power and vulnerability at work.
I welcome music and rhythm, pattern and beauty,
dipping and twisting in cheerful surrender,
partaking in this wonderful gift of living.

May I not be constrained by an aesthetic or image,
nor hindered by the bridle of self-consciousness,
but may I move with graceful indignity—
allowing my body to express my soul's worship.

For what is dance if not a celebration of the body and
        its Creator?
An expression that we are here and whole and real—
or at least, on our way to becoming so?

What is dance if not a beautiful trust fall into freedom?
A flying, leaping, crowd-surfing dependence
on the Living Spirit of love?

Oh God who delights in the offering of dance,
who connects with us through tactility,
who gave us bodies to experience the abundance of life—
teach us to be boundless in beauty,
fathomless in freedom,
resplendent in radiance,
and generous in joy.

Amen.

2 Samuel 6:16–22 • Psalm 30:11–12; 149:3–6; 150 • Zephaniah 3:17 • 1 Corinthians 6:19–20 • 2 Corinthians 3:17

A Blessing for
Dressing for the Day

Oh child of God, in this daily ritual,
may you remember your body is inseparable from
         your soul.

Even in these small tasks, the Most High meets you.

Clothed in Christ, your body is a sacred site,
a cathedral in which the Spirit dwells.
Remember that your faith is an embodied one,
that our incarnate God has placed tremendous value
         on you.

Clothes may be a result of the fall,
but the Lord has redeemed them with colors
and textures
and patterns
and choice.

Our clothing becomes a covering from a merciful and
          tender God.

In selecting your attire,
practice creative expression
and choose clothes that will not hinder your freedom.
Do not live in the extremes of laxity or legalism.
Enjoy these outward symbols of
your Creator-designed self.

At the same time, ask yourself each morning:
Is my body not more important than clothes?

No shirt,
no pants,
no shoes will make you more or less beloved.
For even the fields, dressed in lilies, are clothed better
          than us.

Try radical rebellion against a world
that says you're a number,
that reduces you to size.

Clothe yourself in compassion,
dress in kindness,
drape on humility,
fasten gentleness,
and adorn patience.

Then secure yourself in love
so you can go out and do the same for others.

Amen.

Genesis 3:21 • Matthew 6:25–34 • Luke 12:23 • 1 Corinthians 6:19–20 • Colossians 3:12–14 • 1 Peter 3:3–4

For the Heart

THE TERRAIN OF THE human heart is vast. The heart traverses valleys of anger, plains of friendship, crests of love, and deserts of grief—sometimes all at once. How can something as quiet as your beating heart be so complex and so powerful yet so fragile?

The heart is the seat of hope. Therefore, direct your heart—your hope—toward what is true, what is good, and what is lovely. Be conscious of what you treasure, for hope can be worn thin by disappointment and the heart hardened by misuse. Keep your heart guarded, but do not keep it stagnant. Let it be searched. Let your heart break, if it must, for this brings God close. Let it be remade, from stone into flesh.

Love is not ownership. If love depends on possession, then there is no freedom, only fear of loss. And we know there is no fear in love. To love fully will change you. To be loved wholly will, in turn, change you even more. To give ourselves over to love means to be in relationship with those who have the power to hurt us: friends, parents, partners, co-workers, strangers, even our own selves. To choose to love, even when pain looms as a very real outcome, is to step into the wholeness of our calling, to imitate our Savior—the greatest lover we know.

A Liturgy for a
Broken Heart

Oh Lord,
You have made us soft creatures,
with hearts tender enough to love
and tender enough to break.

How dreadfully painful
and unequivocally beautiful it is to love.

I wish that loving did not mean leaving,
that cherishing did not mean letting go.

But as I heal from this love that did not last,
may the weight and ache of sorrow
press me, pleasantly, into Your chest.

May the loveliness of melancholy come sharply into view,
for You make even sadness beautiful.

May this loss of love not steal my hope
or discourage me from believing the best
or make me callous to the gift of telling someone exactly
              what they mean to me.

Though my heart stings with fresh wounds,
You hold me secure in the reality that I am loved.

In You, all things are healed and held together.
In You, I am both broken-hearted and completely whole.
With You by my side, I acknowledge this pain
and invite it to do its work.

If you find yourself holding
the delicate remains of your heart,
may you realize your strength
and the priceless value of your tenderness
as you receive this blessing below,
honoring what was broken
and hoping in the wholeness to come.

Whether it has been a day or years
since your heart was first hurt,
whether it slowly cracked over time
or shattered all at once,
may you realize that wholeness is still possible,
for you have loved with your entire being,
and to love generously is the greatest gift you can give.

Now is the time to receive:
        to cease striving and know that you are being looked after.

Now is the time to drink deeply of God's healing elixirs:
>   *the sun on your skin,*
>   *the whimsy of birdsongs,*
>   *the shadows shifting under cloud cover,*
>   *the pitter-patter of rain outside your window.*

Now is the time to simply be,
>   *and belong,*
>   *and be loved*
>   *by the One who loved you first.*

May you be radiant with adoration for the God who binds up
>   *your wounds.*
May what was once your greatest hurt become your greatest healing.
May the beauty and power of kindness not be stolen from you.
May you love again.

Take heart, dear one—
for broken-heartedness will not make you less,
it will make you whole.

Amen.

Psalm 34; 46:10 • Isaiah 57:15 • John 15:12–13 • 1 John 3:1; 4:19

A Liturgy for Anger

Oh Lord, Your anger is pure and slowly kindled,
    laced with compassion,
    infused with love.

You do not overlook injustice
    or ignore corruption within Your created order.
You hear the groans of the innocent
    and are grieved by the mistreatment of Your
        beloved.
Your voice thunders when worship is given
    to anything that cannot handle its weight.

Thank You for this ability to feel, deep in our gut,
when something is not right,
when circumstances require resolution,
when wounds need healing.

But we need Your help, oh Lord,
for the spark of irritation becomes a fire of destruction
when it burns with unchecked rage.

May the flame of fury destroy only what is unjust
and harm no one in the process.
May the blaze of indignation be directed toward
      wrongdoing
and not toward a human soul.

While we are angry,
    may we not lose faith in You.
While we are angry,
    may we not fall out of step with Your Spirit.
While we are angry,
    may we not seek revenge
but rely on You to restore all that has been taken away.

Oh Lord, anger is often a shield we raise
to protect ourselves from sorrow,
from wounds yet unhealed,
but may we trust You enough to let You behind our guards,
inviting You into our tender places of unbearable pain.

Come, Lord Jesus.

Amen.

Numbers 14:18 • Psalm 37:8–11 • Proverbs 14:29 • Micah 7:18–19 • Isaiah 57:16–19
• Romans 1:18 • Ephesians 4:26–32 • 1 Thessalonians 5:9–11

A Liturgy for Waiting for a Response After Putting Yourself Out There

Oh God of risky love,
I have made myself vulnerable to another,
and the tenderness of my feelings has been laid bare.

There is something wildly thrilling
and completely terrifying
and deeply right about living with clear intentions—
about choosing boldness at the proper time.

Thank You for this opportunity to be brave,
for this chance to pursue what is beautiful and
worthwhile.
Thank You that You have given me this soft heart
that is not afraid to love, to risk, to ask.

Oh my Redeemer,
may I release the control of this outcome to You,

not attempting to pressure Your beloved into doing what
       I want
but giving them complete freedom to choose for
       themselves.

May I wait patiently for their answer
and celebrate this opportunity to know them better.

May the person I have opened my heart to
steward well the tenderness I have entrusted to them.

But even if they do not,
if my heart gets dismissed or mishandled,
spread Your wings of comfort and compassion over me.

Surround me with safe people
to be gentle with my heart if it bruises.
Surround me with a community who will encourage me
as You make me stronger and wiser than before.

May I remember that an offering of love is an act of
       kindness,
astonishingly beautiful whether or not it is received.

Amen.

Genesis 29:1–30 • Ruth 3:1–18 • Esther 8:1–17 • Song of Songs 8:6–7 • 1 John 4:7–19

A Liturgy for Falling in Love

Oh God, I am falling in love, and it shows.

Flustered and thrilled,
scattered and delighted,
I am swirling with new emotions
and fresh dreams.

Thank You for this stirring of my soul,
for the evidence of my beating, living heart.

Thank You for these flutters of anticipation,
for the physical reminders of Your Spirit's work within me.

There is an agony here as well,
an unnameable ache as this love feels outsized to my
                frame.

I live with one foot in this glorious present
and one in the imagined future,
where there exists a multitude of directions this could go.
Heart-consumed, I kneel before You,
asking for wisdom to navigate whatever may come.

First, protect my hope, God of strength.
Guard it fiercely and show me how to do the same.

I boldly ask—
if You are willing—
for this relationship to last, oh Giver of good things.

Cultivate joy and light in this relationship, oh God.
When my desire overwhelms, help me to love with dignity.
May our togetherness say something true about the gospel,
about the glory of our greater Lover.

Burn away my idealism, for there is no human
who can grant me the fullness I already have in You.

Braid us into rich, honest community with others,
with friends who see and know us,
who carry us always to the cross.

You know, oh Lord, how I long
for the safety of covenant with this person,
for the mysterious unity of marriage.
But until You stir and awaken us to this reality,
I will wait.

And if You tell me to leave,
if this is not whom I can give lifelong commitment to,
I will need Your courage to let go.

Most of all, oh First Love,
remind me of Your perfect affection.
You will not be led off the path in Your pursuit of me.
You will not relent in Your passion.
May nothing overshadow this love You have for me
and my love for You.

Amen.

Psalm 23:6; 27:14 • Proverbs 3:5–6 • Ecclesiastes 4:12 • Song of Songs 8:4 • Romans 15:13 • James 1:5

A Blessing for Loving
When You Don't Feel It

When your warmth toward another has cooled,
love anyway.

When you feel distance has grown between you,
love anyway.

When you have forgotten the fever of a heart on fire,
love anyway.

When you feel guarded,
give love lavishly instead,
and remember you, too, need the grace to receive it back.

Now is the time to become soft again,
to choose gentleness over record-keeping
and tenderness over apathy.

In doing so, you are not faking it,
but rather trusting the Spirit will complete this act of love.

Ask God to release the dam
so the currents of adoration can flow once again.

May your hands and words be safe.
May you always assume the best of the other.

If you long to recall the song you once sung,
remember that love perseveres
and ask for new sweetness to come.

Swim out to the depths you have forged together
and explore what you have forgotten.

Find glory in the quiet,
magic in the commonplace,
playfulness in the boredom,
and passion in the everyday pursuit of each other.

Notice, with gratitude, how love binds everything back
          together.

Amen.

Psalm 103:14 • Isaiah 40:8 • Luke 12:27–28 • 1 Corinthians 13 • Philippians 2:3 •
Colossians 3:14

A Liturgy for Forgiving
a Parent

Father, forgive my parent
and help me do the same.

Through my parent's actions—
or inaction—
I have not believed I am beloved.

While other children are the apple of their parents' eyes,
protected above all else,
I am left wanting,
hurt by the complex conditions of their love.

While other children walk green pastures with their parents,
I reside in a minefield.

Father, forgive my parent
and help me do the same.

In this disappointment,
I find dependence on You, Abba.
Show me how to bless and not curse.
Keep my pain from twisting into resentment,
from becoming a knife that lives in my own chest.

As I lie awake, rehashing this hurt,
comfort me with the knowledge
that no teardrop falls uncounted by You.

I know, Lord of infinite mercy, that
forgiveness comes from being forgiven.
Bring to mind the ways You have pulled me from the pit,
the days in which Your salvation was my only hope.

Father, forgive me
so I can do the same.

Reveal where I've held my parent to a standard
no one could meet but You.
Idealized and idolized, no human could
stand under the weight of my expectations.

I long to be understood,
cherished,
and esteemed by my family,
but I entrust myself to You,
who will not forsake me.

In the future,
in a plot twist of grace,

I believe time will give me new eyes to see what's hidden,
what is blurred by my hurt.
Until then, I can rest knowing that You,
who judge justly, are at work,
always in pursuit of my parent.

So Father, forgive my parent
and help me do the same.

Amen.

Psalm 10:17–18; 17:8; 27:10–14 • Luke 18:7–8; 23:34 • Romans 12:14 • Ephesians 4:31–32 • Colossians 3:13 • 1 Peter 2:21–23

A Liturgy for Healthy Boundaries

Oh God, there are limits to what I can do,
what I can give,
what I can withstand.
In honoring my finitude,
I release control to You.

Longing to be everything to everyone,
I have said *yes* when I meant *no.*
Grant me discernment to guard this heart
from being trampled.
Show me the lines around my life
that have fallen in pleasant places.

Reveal the boundaries that will keep me
closer to my Savior.
Even You, Jesus, spent time away to be with the Father.

Spirit, I strive to stay where You stay
and leave when You lead.
Leaving can be holy when You're at the helm,
like an exodus from chains I was never meant to wear.

The gift of my vulnerability is not for everyone,
but at the same time, oh God,
I know no one is exempt from love.

Oh Christ, may my boundaries not be placed so high
they become a fortress,
an impenetrable wall that turns my soul to stone.

May my boundaries not deter corrections made in love,
for the wounds from a friend can be trusted.

And, above all, may my boundaries not become an excuse
        or avoidance
but rather set me up to prioritize my purpose,
to further Your kingdom,
to live wholeheartedly for You.

Amen.

Psalm 16:6 • Matthew 5:37; 7:6, 15 • Luke 5:15–16

For the Soul

CONSIDER THE LAST TIME your soul was stirred: the way something made you tremor with joy, pause with reverence, or lean into mystery. Then consider the last time your soul was wounded: the way something made you recoil in pain, retreat from others, or question your beliefs. In matters of the soul, your whole self is involved.

Your soul—your inmost being, knit together fearfully and wonderfully—is the totality of you: your body, your feelings, your imagination, your longings, your limitations, your memories, your convictions, your affections. To speak of your soul is to speak of your life. Your entire being, with all of its inclinations and desires, is your offering. And every day, as you walk the streets or drive on roads, eat around tables or shake another's hand, you encounter other souls, those full selves sustained by the same One as you.

Tend to your soul as one stokes a fire. Keep the embers from

89

becoming ash. Ask the questions with no immediate answers. Mark new seasons. Reach for the Friend you miss. Grieve the dreams that died, then turn and celebrate what never came to pass. Allow your soul—your truest self—to find union with its Creator.

A Liturgy for Accepting
Yourself as You Are

Oh Lord,
what a marvel it is to exist,
to be alive,
to embody a soul that is beloved by You.

You have given me a body—*this* body,
exactly as it is, on purpose, for a purpose.

You have given me a mind—*this* mind,
bursting with unique thoughts, spinning with new ideas.

You have given me a soul—*this* soul,
to be tender to Your presence,
to connect with You in intimate ways.

What an honor it is to bear Your image,
to explore the depths and edges of human nature.

By my very existence,
I am brought closer to You.
By my very existence,
Your mysteries are manifested
and Your wonders worshipped.

But how easy it is to criticize my created self,
to wish that it were different,
more like another.
How common for the clay to tell the Potter what it
        should be.

Oh Creator of my character,
give me eyes to see myself the way that You see me,
apart from the brokenness of my sin.
Impart to me the vision that compelled You to create me.
Let me view my idiosyncrasies with pleasure,
my physical features with reverence,
my imperfections with grace.

Expose what hinders me from accepting myself as I am
so that the gifts you have embedded deep within me
come pouring out in abundance.

I may not possess every trait that I wish,
but I am whole—
an exquisite creature of your imagination.

How fun it is to be myself!
How delightful to embrace my quirks
and explore my full potential.

As I move forward in the world,
may I experience a wholeness so freeing
that I forget to be encumbered with myself.
I fully expect and earnestly hope
that I will not at all be ashamed.

Amen.

Psalm 34:5; 139:1–5, 16 • Isaiah 45:9–13; 64:8 • 1 Corinthians 6:19–20 • Philippians 1:20 • Philippians 3:1–14

A Liturgy for Those Who Don't Know What They Believe

To the One whose name I'm not sure I know,
I yearn for the days when belief was easy,
when answers seemed simple,
when doubts did not swarm my thinking.

The faith I once followed without question feels foreign,
and the convictions I once held with certainty
do not seem as black-and-white as before.

I am frightened by these unknowns
and unsettled by my own skepticism,
dreading the rejection of my community
and stunned by the thought of losing You.

In this moment of existential upheaval,
would You remember me,
even if I cannot remember You?

Would You have mercy on my humanity
and the fragile limits of my understanding?

Would You remind me that you are intimately acquainted
with the formation of my mind and heart,
and that You have deep compassion
on all that You have made?

If You are truly God,
then You are not shaken when beliefs change.
You are in control of it all.

You are not alarmed by my questions.
You are not angry with my doubts.
Perhaps You are sovereignly leading me into
deeper trust,
deeper wisdom,
deeper faith.

You are not housed in religions made by humans,
but live in the wild freedom of Your creation
as it lives and dies and sings to You.
You are not served by robotic devotion
but delight in hearts who are so desperate to touch You
that they will wrestle You to the ground.

May I be fascinated by all I do not yet know
and all that You want to show me.

May I continue to imperfectly reach for You,
even if it looks different from the way it did before.

May my expectations and imagination stretch beyond
        myself,
as I become pleasurably small and dependent on You,
lifting my eyes with nothing to prove.

May I keep being honest with You,
even if I cannot fully grasp You.
And when I'm not sure where I'm going,
may I dare to hope that You are not far away.

Amen.

Psalm 103; 139:10 • Acts 17:24–28 • James 4:7–8

A Liturgy for New Seasons of Life

As summer turns to fall
and winter turns to spring,
we watch the world seed and sprout,
blossom and diminish—
thriving in this divinely created order.

And so it is with our lives.

We know it is necessary, Lord,
for the old to give way to the new,
but it pains us to watch what we grew fade away,
for we cannot see this new thing You are doing
and can only grieve what is coming to an end.

Yet even in this uncertainty,
on the brink of beginnings,
we ask You to bless this transition

and the discomfort that accompanies it.
Bless the grief for what is ending
as well as the anticipation of what is to come.
Bless the restlessness,
the uprooting and the replanting,
for it is training us in reliance on You.

If this season looks different from those around us,
may we not be discouraged but curious
to see the unique goodness You have stored up for us.

If this season is unwanted,
a step back instead of a step forward,
may we remember that You make everything beautiful in
        its time
and weave all things together for good,
beckoning us deeper into Your purpose and glory.

If this season feels stagnant,
the same-old, same-old,
a discouraging dose of "Is this all there is?"—
may we remember that You give life to the full,
bestowing generous gifts when we least expect them.

Thank You, Lord, that though our seasons change,
You remain the same—
yesterday, today, and forever.
May we build our lives on You,
our solid rock,
our firm foundation,
who does not change with shifting shadows.

Draw us out into the wild,

into the places we cannot yet see.

May we not be afraid of uncharted realms,

but thrilled for the adventures they hold.

May we creatively seek You in this new season,

led forth by mystery into the house of wonder.

Amen.

Psalm 31:19; 100:5 • Ecclesiastes 3:1–8, 11 • John 10:10 • Romans 8:28 • Ephesians 2:10 • Hebrews 13:8 • James 1:17

A Liturgy for
the Lukewarm

Oh God, I miss burning for You.

My first Love feels like a memory faded,
a story I cannot quite remember.
Straddling devotion and departure,
I still claim You and yet my life does not reflect
            this.

As one misses a friend,
so I long for a word from Your mouth,
for uninterrupted time at Your side.
Though I do not feel close with You as I once did,
Your very being still shadows my days,
still haunts my thoughts,
still chases me down.
Who else knows me as You do?

Consume me once again.

Stir the tepid waters of my heart.

Do not relent in Your steadfast pursuit.

Give me an intolerance toward disconnection with You,

toward anything less than life-giving loyalty.

May obedience to You feel less like drudgery

and more like love.

I am a witness to your faithfulness

and a recipient of Your kindness,

an empty cistern You have filled before.

Awaken me, oh God!

Awake, my soul!

Giver of life, I cling to the resurrection,

to the hope that You will restore what feels dead.

Father of love, release me from passionless duty

and lead me deeper into joy,

into the reality of intimacy.

For You are the Lover who waits up for me,

who leaves the light on,

who runs to welcome me back home, again and again.

Amen.

Psalm 23:6 • Matthew 9:16–17; 16:26 • Luke 15:11–32 • James 3:10–12 • 1 John 4:18
• Revelation 3:15–16

In Praise of
Unanswered Prayers

All praise to the One who heard my prayer
and did not answer the way I wanted.

All praise to the One who sees what I cannot,
whose knowledge transcends time and
the variability of the human heart.

All praise to the One who sometimes grants the gift of
        hindsight,
who gently turns us toward what could have been
and reveals what He spared us from.

Lord, I look at the map of my life and see how
the twisting roads,
the shadowed valleys, and the dead ends
led me here.
You did not answer every prayer,

but I've gained something greater:
trust, perseverance, and closeness with You.
A faith refined by refusal and worth more than gold.
Guarded by Your denial,
I see the necessary protection in Your *no*.

Holy One of mystery, I know the pleasure You take
in persistent prayers,
in our pleas of honesty and baring of desires.
I also believe You see it all,
that You alone know how the outcomes of my prayers
affect more than I can comprehend.
Sometimes Your *no* to me
is a *yes* to someone else.

If it is true You withhold no good thing,
then there is mercy in this lack,
in the ache of a desire unfulfilled.

I am grateful for the clarity of distance.
Funny how the thing I once longed for with my entire self
is now but a speck of dust,
a period at the end of a sentence I cannot remember.

I now step forward with the grace of looking backward
and believing You are good.
I cannot know everything else,
but I trust that I am loved.

Amen.

Psalm 84:11 • James 4:3 • 1 John 5:14

A Liturgy for Grieving the Loss
of Something You Never Had

God of comfort, how can I mourn for something that was
      never mine?

The future I imagined has turned to dust,
and this dream, once beautiful, is gone.
Though it was never mine to begin with,
my life still feels interrupted,
upended,
by this loss.

But because I mourn as one with hope,
I will choose to look grief in the face without shame,
to believe lamenting is obedience
and a testament to my working heart.

Jesus who once wept,
I turn to Your empty tomb,

to You who defied the grave,
and trust that, through You, the death of this dream will
            not destroy me.

And yet, though I long for the day
when this sting is but ancient history,
this wound may sometimes weep fresh.
Though the nature of my loss feels abstract
and difficult to describe,
I trust that You, Man of Sorrows, understand
and will always hold me fast.

Guard my heart against hardening
and protect it from illusions of future disappointment,
for to lose hope would be to add sorrow upon sorrow.

As I let You tend to this real pain,
help me not to forever pine after what You have not given,
but to take hold of the life I have.
Help me to live, more than ever,
with the wholeness found in You.

Amen.

Psalm 84:11 • Isaiah 42:3; 53:3 • Matthew 5:4 • John 11:35 • 2 Corinthians 1:3–5 •
1 Thessalonians 4:13–14

A Blessing for Bravery

Child of God, fear has built its barricade in your road.
As your heart races at the unknown,
determine to see what lies on the other side.
When your hands shake and your knees sway,
show up sweaty and stay, even if you tremble.
Tilt your head not inward but upward.
Lean into the God who has never stopped sustaining you,
who is worthy of your trust.

Become wary of the voice that says *safety lies in fear.*
If reason keeps you bound, embrace gumption,
trusting the gentle voice urging you on
more than the swirling shriek of *what-ifs.*
Move toward the unknown, crawling if you cannot stride.
Believe—even weakly—that courage is freedom.

Be brave if it means saying *yes*.
Be brave if it means saying *no*.
Be brave because you are loved.
Take the risk without expectation of shame,
for even if you fall down flat, the Lord will meet you on
        the ground.

To stand brave and open-hearted on this earth is nothing
        short of a miracle,
nothing less than taking Jesus at His word.
If He has already overcome the troubles of this world,
then so, too, have you.
This is the promise on which we stand:
our story is not over with failure, with scorn, with pain.
We are free to live and love and move
as if we have already conquered everything we fear.

What if greater joy is found in the unknown?
What if life is found in the mystery?
What if at the end of our courage is not success or failure
but rather Jesus Himself?

Child of God, take one step more and see what lies on the
        other side.

Amen.

Psalm 121 • John 16:33 • Romans 8:18 • Philippians 1:20; 4:6–7 • 2 Timothy 1:7

For the Home

BELIEVE THAT WHOLENESS IS possible in the home you are building—be it an apartment, a house, or a shared space with roommates. Set your table and watch as it becomes a place of nourishment and joy. Welcome friends and family through your front door and absorb their kindness into your walls. May your pain find a resting place, a healing sanctuary, as God establishes for you a home that exudes life. For you are alive and becoming more so each day.

Bring your broken pieces to the table; they are welcome here. Do not run from the ways your former homes hurt you, but grieve them so you might release them. Acknowledge what they gave you or did not give you. Expose your memories to the light and begin to make new ones. Pull up old carpets and lay down new floors. Hang what is pleasing and memorable on your walls. Do not be ashamed if it's different. Do not be ashamed if it's you. One brick at a time, begin to build a home that is safe for yourself and others, and then open the doors. Pull up the chairs. See where you have more than you need and give those margins away.

A Liturgy for Weary Parents

Abba Father,
You have entrusted me with children
to feed and clothe,
to train and discipline,
to cultivate with care and curiosity.

I know this calling is a blessing—
one that You are using to make me more like You.
But sometimes I wish I could press pause and breathe,
to allow my mind to catch up with my feet,
to give my body the rest it needs.

I am weary from stewarding
this beautiful gift of my child's life.

But if weariness is Your preferred stage
on which to display Your power,

then come, Holy Father,
to the stage of my weakness.
My exhaustion does not disappoint You.
My fatigue does not frighten You.
My apathy is only proof that I am human.

I have no strength to muster up for You.
I can only tell You this is hard.

Would You join me in my weariness, now?

As I continue to put one foot in the front of the
            other,
may I persevere with eyes locked on You
instead of my dwindling energy supply.
You are with me even when I feel unseen.

May I sense—deep in my soul—that You carry me
when I have nothing left to give.

You will restore my resources.
You will renew my strength.
There will be days when parenting is not this hard,
when joy will erupt and laughter will resound,
but today, I bring my weariness as an offering to You.

Here are the worn-out parts of my body.
Here are the shreds of my energy.
Here are the chaotic bits of my home.
Here are the circumstances I can't control.

May these tattered but wholehearted sacrifices please You.

Amen.

Psalm 51:17; 127:3–5 • Isaiah 40:31 • Matthew 11:28–30 • John 15:4 • Romans 12:1–2 • 2 Corinthians 12:9–10

A Liturgy for an Ordinary
Day at Home

God of the everyday,
God of the ordinary,
God who saturates our simplicity with significance.

Our days are made up of moments—
unglamorous and unimpressive—
that when added together, form a life.

As we make and remake the bed,
wash the dishes only to dirty them again,
fold clothes only to wear them the next day,
we wonder—can what is mundane be sacred?

We desire adventure, not routine,
for the extraordinary to outshine the common,
for day-to-day rituals to be steeped in splendor.

But, Lord, in Your kindness, remind us how
You have woven the glory we long for into our every day.
You have infused our cluttered kitchens,
our sticky countertops,
our leaky faucets
with meaning.

Open our eyes to the depths that are before us.
Show us how daily walks can lead to profound worship,
how preparing a meal can be a conversation with You,
how organizing the fridge,
and sorting the mail,
and cleaning old pens out of the junk drawer
can hold hidden snippets of joy,
if we will only look for them.

May we become like children on a treasure hunt,
eyes wide with eagerness and expectation.

May we greet every ordinary day with curiosity and
                fascination,
ears tuned to the way Your voice whispers to us
from the corners of a messy room.

Father, You not only display Your glory
in the wild wonders of nature,
but You tuck it into pockets and couch cushions,
waiting to surprise us with unforeseen beauty.

May we delight in these mustard seeds of majesty together,
for life with You is simple and sweet and erupting
    with eternity.

Amen.

Psalm 19:1–2; 27:4; 63; 84; 131:1–2 • Matthew 6:30–33

A Liturgy for a New Parent

Keeper of children,
You have given me a wonderful gift.

I have imagined these first days
and dreamt of this face,
yet no wondering or planning
could have prepared me for the reality of my baby,
for the multiplication of our family
and expansion of my heart.

This child is not a duplicate of myself
but rather their own person,
a whole creation woven together by You,
chosen and dear.
Your thoughts for them
already outnumber the grains of sand.

117

I marvel at this example of Your workmanship.
I gaze in wonder at Your handiwork.

Thrilled by this miracle
but overwhelmed in my exhaustion,
my comfortable routines have been upended by this
        small life.

Rid me of shame, God,
if the complexity of emotions threatens to topple me.
Excited and disoriented,
grateful and grieving my sense of self,
I feel strung between paradox.
I trust You to steer me in the shock of parenthood.

Great Sustainer, restore me with sleep and strength.
Show mercy in my upside-down routine.
Give me blessings to pray over this cherished one.
Jesus, who gathered children in Your arms,
be with me in the sweetness of holding my baby,
of feeling their head rest against my heart.

Embodying dependence,
this newborn reminds me to become more like
        a child,
just as You have called us to be.

God who became a baby,
You once entrusted Your own self to human parents,
Your newborn cries an eternal echo of
the vulnerability of the young.

We live in a world of both beauty and brutality,
one I cannot imagine this small soul stumbling into.
My heart has grown little legs
that will one day carry forth onto the earth,
to walk and eat and learn and love.

Because You live, oh Jesus, my child can face whatever
      comes.
May pointing them to You be my greatest goal.

Amen.

Psalm 139 • Mark 10:13–16 • Ephesians 2:10

A Liturgy for Roommates

Meet us in our home, oh Jesus, as we offer it back
    to You.

Make this place a respite,
a sanctuary,
a haven for those who enter.

Oh Lord, loneliness was the first thing You called
    not good,
so we thank You for each other.
We do not want to take for granted this companionship.
Create in us a friendship that lasts beyond these
    walls,
and may the sweetness of unity mark our days.

We each have our own routines,
so help them to sync instead of clash.

Grant us grace in extra measure during busy
      weeks
and steady rhythms in quiet ones.

When we hear the garage door open or the jingle of keys
      in the door,
may the sound of the other's arrival be a blessing instead
      of a burden.

In times when we are ships in the night,
may the way we care for shared space speak, "You are
      loved."

Even in passing,
may our words cover each other in warmth,
always building up and never tearing down.
May we be ready to listen,
quick to offer prayer in place of platitudes,
unhurried enough to see each other's heart.

Stir us to default to honor,
to service,
to ready apologies,
and to forgiveness.
Teach us to resolve conflict together,
and let nothing be uttered behind backs
that we would not say to Christ's beloved ones.

May the melody of laughter,
the stillness of peace,
and the aroma of harmony fill our home

and float out our door,
so even our neighbors experience the Light
        inside.

May we feel blessed, oh Lord, by the way we belong here
        with You.

Amen.

Genesis 2:18 • Romans 12:10, 16 • Galatians 5:22–23 • Ephesians 4:1–3 • Philippians 2:1–4

A Liturgy for Those
Who Live Alone

Oh Jesus, who often spent time in solitude,
teach me how to live alone well.

As the only one responsible for this home,
I can become dizzy with decision-making.
Guide me with Your wisdom, Wonderful Counselor,
and be the first One I always consult.

Whether it was my choice or not,
this solo life affords autonomy, but with my privacy and
        freedom
comes an ache for the warmth of a nearby soul.

In this overpowering silence,
be my listening ear, oh God,
and hear the stories from my day.

Join me as I cook my meals
and clean my messes.
Protect and comfort me as I sleep alone.

When I catch my own reflection,
over and over again,
help me not to grow so accustomed to loneliness
that I forget I was made to be loved.

I do not want to take for granted
the gifts in this arrangement,
wallowing with abandon or
turning wasteful and selfish with resources.
Instead, grant me the desire to open my door
        often,
flinging it wide for those in need,
growing generous with my space and time,
choosing to say, "You are welcome here."

May my home become a haven for others,
a sanctuary for guests to breathe deeply of Your
        love.
And when they leave, help me to relish solitude,
to notice Your voice,
to lean against You,
for You are always available to commune with.

Because, oh Jesus, You have already made Your home
        with us—
in me—

I can settle ever deeper here,
sure that wherever I live, so too will You.

Amen.

Psalm 4:8 • Proverbs 17:1 • Romans 12:13 • 1 Peter 4:9; 5:7

A Liturgy for
Washing Your Face

Oh Living Water, join me as I wash my face,
for the smallest of acts are seen by You.

Even the tedious routines can be holy,
so make this sink an altar at which I may encounter You,
      oh Lord.

Wash me with these streams of water,
cleansing me of everything not from You.

As I scrub my skin, purify my heart.
As I clean my body, reveal me as a new creation.
As I splash and dry, make this soap an offering, a pleasing
      aroma,
and turn my face to You, oh Christ.

Where shadows of sorrow and shame cloud my eyes,
may my face now reflect Your radiance.
Anoint me with oil so that I may overflow.

As I wash at the start of morning,
refresh and strengthen me for what lies ahead.
As I wash before bed,
move the day's mistakes and mishaps down the drain,
so I may receive Your gift of sleep with peace.

May I notice how You join me in the mundane.
May even this scrubbing become a prayer.

Repeat these words at the end of your washing:

Oh God, may the sacredness of this ritual
and time spent with You
restore me for whatever lies ahead.

Amen.

Psalm 23:5; 34:5; 51:7 • Isaiah 61:1 • Matthew 6:17

A Blessing for a Dinner Party

Gather around the table,
you who are hungry and healing.
Gather around the bread and wine,
you fellows and kindred.
Gather shoulder to shoulder,
you weary travelers,
with those who have crossed your path
on this journey home.

As you take your seat at the table,
warmed by comradery and candlelight,
may you come as you truly are,
without shame or reservation,
leaving all performance at the door.

As you ease into the comfort of food
and the candor of conversation,

may the weights and worries you have carried here
slip easily off your shoulders.

As you satiate your hunger and thirst,
may you remember your spiritual needs
and be fed—both body and soul.

May water cleanse you
and wine refresh you.
May bread nourish you
and flavors fascinate you.
May the riches of food and friendship
be the bounty that you feast upon.

As you linger with other guests,
may you know the deep joy
and even deeper satisfaction
of belonging.

As you raise your glasses,
may you give honor to all who surround you,
for everyone who partakes in this meal
is a masterpiece of creation.

And may the Spirit of God—
who teaches us the delights
of true communion—
come join us.

Amen.

Psalm 36:8; 63:5 • Isaiah 55:1–2 • Mark 14:22–26 • Luke 14:15–23 • John 4:14; 6:35

For the Community

BEAR WITNESS TO THE fullness of another's life. Learn through their stories: their heartbreak and their dreams, their homes and their meals. Notice the new facets of God revealed through your neighbors, your co-workers, your friends, or your cashier at the grocery store. Loneliness was the first thing that was named *not good,* and perhaps it's because communion with God means communion with others.

We cannot love someone without knowing them, and we cannot know them from afar. We know our neighbors through conversation. We know our friends through breaking bread. We know our community by choosing commitment over convenience, by staying through difficulty, by participating in the life around us. You may have to forge a community instead of stumbling upon it. In knowing and loving others, we hope for the delight and dignity of being known and loved ourselves. For community, in its fullest form, is people echoing our Creator's intention to one another: *Here is the world, and you belong.*

A Liturgy of Gratitude
for Your Community

Oh Founder of friendships and families,
as I journey deeper into this life,
I look around with gratitude
and marvel at the companions
You have chosen to join me along the way.

Thank You for the old friends
who have become pillars in my life
through loyalty and longevity.
Thank You for this foundation, this security,
this trust that has built over time.
Allow us to continue growing together,
as You unveil the unique purposes You have placed within
     us.

Thank You for the new friends—
the ones I wasn't looking for but can't imagine life without.

Thank You that we found each other at just the right time,
making space for one another in our already crowded
       lives.
Thank You that we get to explore life together—
the beauty as well as the pain we meet along the way.
May new friendships become powerful partnerships—
deep and lasting and rich.

Thank You for the uncommon kindred
who add dimension to our every day—
for work friends and school friends,
for neighborhood friends and park friends,
for parents and kids,
for nieces and nephews,
for the families that form with or without biological ties.
Though they may not be our daily companions,
their presence sweetens the spaces they occupy.

Help me remember that it is good and right
for communities to change with time.
I thank You for my community as it is today,
as it used to be,
and as it will be in the future.

May I surround myself with people who feel like
       home,
who help me heal and grow,
who help me love and learn.
Knit our hearts tightly together
as we continue to spur one another on

toward goodness and integrity
and the love that is better than life.

Amen.

Psalm 63:3 • Romans 12:9–10 • Philippians 2:1–4 • Colossians 3:12–17 • Hebrews 10:24

A Liturgy for Those Who Are Afraid to Meet Their Neighbors

Oh Lord,
We want to love You with our whole selves—
our bodies and souls, our hearts and minds—
and to treat our neighbors with profound significance,
not out of obligation or performance,
but because each of them has been formed by You.

We admit that others' quirks—
their peculiar habits and homes—
can tempt us to withdraw,
forsaking pursuit and forfeiting connection.

Instead of seeing our neighbors as an inconvenience,
would You fill us with awe for the people You have made?

Would You highlight whom You have placed in our path
        to know,

and show us the needs we are well suited to meet?
For perhaps we have been put in our neighbor's path
for a holy purpose,
even if it is just to remember
that abundant life involves the continual symbiosis
of caring for one another.

May we approach our neighbors with cheerful generosity,
and may our words and actions be soothing to their
       wounds.
May we welcome each other with a smile,
and may our kindness be an invitation into freedom.
May fear and hesitancy become a distant memory,
and may mercy and care become second nature,
as we reach out to connect and show honor,
communicating that we are simply here to love.

Amen.

Matthew 22:35–40 • Luke 10:25–37 • 1 Corinthians 10:24 • 1 John 4:18

A Liturgy for Loving
Your Enemies

Oh Author of Love,

It is easy to love those who love us back,
trusting in the safe and familiar,
showing kindness to those who show kindness
        to us.
But You have shocked us with an opposite way—
    one that shows mercy to our enemies
    and compassion to those who mistreat us.

How can this be, Lord,
when the need for protection is so great
and the cry for justice will not be silenced?

We cannot help but ask,
Do You care that we have been harmed and cheated?
Do You care that we have been bewildered and humiliated?

Look upon us now in our anger and disillusionment.
We hold our enemies up to You, and say, *Look! Hear! Help!*
Something must be done, and we trust You to do what
      is right.

In the meantime, we call to mind the mistreatment
that Christ endured at the hands of His own community.
We call to mind His sacrifice that made wrong things right,
His surrendered trust in the Father,
His acceptance of beating and mockery
with resurrection right around the corner.

May we follow Your example
and make space in our hearts
for those who believe differently,
speak differently,
see differently—
even if these differences offend us.
May we not villainize each other with our disagreements
but seek to understand before we are understood.

Oh Lord, we place the burden of justice upon Your
      shoulders
and leave the responsibility of revenge up to You.
Your heart is pure.
Your intentions are good.
Your love is fierce and sees all things clearly.

May we trust when You say You will repay
and believe when You say You will restore what has been
      taken away.

May we care for our enemies and meet their needs,

no longer fighting evil with evil,

but overpowering evil with good.

Amen.

Psalm 71:20–21 • Isaiah 53:7–10 • Joel 2:25–26 • Matthew 5:38–48 • Romans 12:19–21
• 1 Peter 5:10

A Liturgy for Gentleness
Toward Others

Oh Lamb of God,
who beautifully embodies the gentleness we desire,
teach us Your way of living:
    unhurried yet purposeful,
    humble yet resolute,
    unswayed by the expectations of others
    yet always keeping their best interests at heart.

Would You take us by the hand, Holy Spirit,
and keep us in step with You—
even when someone has wronged us?

Though it seems to be in short supply,
would You show us how gentleness is a force for good,
disarming strongholds of evil
and clearing pathways for peace?

A gentle heart is not a weak heart
but rather one in possession of great power,
caring so deeply for the good of others
that it wields only the necessary amount.

Make us discontent with self-serving superiority
and the instinct to apply excessive force.
Lead us instead into a better reality—
where strength is stewarded delicately
and used to uplift others,
where communities flourish
out of hearts that are free.

As we learn Your way of gentleness, tender Teacher,
may we choose softness over dominance
    and restraint over impulse.
May we seek to understand,
    even while we are misunderstood.
May the harshness of striving
    melt into the ease of rest.
And may the kindness on our tongues
    stop bitterness in its tracks.

When gentleness feels like a fruit we cannot produce,
we welcome Your provision, Lord,
and take our time reconnecting to the Vine.

May Your meekness and gentleness inspire us,
for they are not signs of weakness
but of Your preeminent power and wisdom
under profound control, for the sake of others.

We can do no good apart from You, Lord,

but You give us sufficiency in all things.

So bless the seeds of our efforts,

however small they may be.

Amen.

Proverbs 15:1 • Matthew 11:25–30 • John 15:12–17 • Galatians 5:1–6:10 • Ephesians 4:1–6 • Philippians 2:1–11 • 2 Timothy 2:22–26 • 1 Peter 3:8–12

A Liturgy for Teachers

Oh Jesus, Teacher of all teachers,
join us at school.

On the days we have energy
and burst with ideas,
sure of our calling,
bless our teaching.

On the days we struggle to show up
and feel tired to our core,
questioning our calling,
bless our teaching.

Grant us the grace to know our work is valuable,
that caring for minds and hearts
will bear years of fruit when done in Your name.

Then, give us endurance when our work feels pointless
and our efforts meaningless,
for we need to see how this matters in light of eternity.

Widen our capacity to overcome the chaos of the day
and protect us with perseverance.

When students overwhelm us, may our spirits be patient.
When parents critique us, may our dispositions be kind.
When administrators observe us, may our lessons be
            covered in peace.
When gossip grows, may our words be draped in
            gentleness.
When a student needs our full attention, may our love
            be lavish.

Spark us with creativity, oh perfect Creator,
even within the confines of these lesson plans and rules,
so we can engage our students
and excite their imaginations,
setting Your next generation of ambassadors ablaze.

Protect our students' wonder.
Guard them from cynicism
and disillusionment.
Awaken in them a thirst for righteousness.
May our witness to the gospel
touch everything we teach,
infusing every subject with hope
and pointing to Your complete story.

Keep me ever aware, oh God, that I am still a learner too.

No matter what comes,
as I steward this vocation for the sake of Your kingdom,
may I always believe that You, the God of all hope,
are working everything out for our good.

Amen.

Proverbs 9:9; 22:6 • Romans 5:3–4; 12:6–7 • 2 Corinthians 5:20 • Galatians 5:22–23;
6:6 • Colossians 1:11; 3:16 • Titus 2:7–8 • James 1:2–4

A Liturgy for a Trip
to the Grocery Store

Oh God of abundance, come with me on this grocery
       store trip,
an unremarkable errand You can transform with
divine possibility.

Rid me of haste before I enter the store.
Let my steps down aisles be slow
and my posture toward others be patient.

May this place of overstimulation
that triggers one's greed
somehow become a place of stillness
and self-control.

As I fill my cart with what I need,
remind me that it is You alone who sustain me,

in both body and spirit.
Let me be satisfied by nothing other than You.

Show me the way of good stewardship—
how to spend less on myself
and consider others as I shop.

If anxiety comes as I navigate these aisles,
quiet me with Your presence
and the steadiness of Your hand.

Even here, remind me of the access I have
to the fruit of Your Spirit:
may my love be genuine,
my kindness tireless,
my gentleness unrelenting.

In every encounter with strangers—
cashiers and baggers,
greeters and butchers,
fellow sojourners with carts—
may I treat them with dignity,
for I do not know the griefs with which they
      arrived.

Oh perfect Provider—
for today and every future grocery run—
this is what I ask:
Help me to spend my resources in a way that nourishes
      this body,

blesses others,
and most of all, honors You.

Amen.

Matthew 6:11 • Isaiah 55:2 • 1 Corinthians 10:31

A Liturgy for Those Who Feel Behind in Life

God who sees and knows me,
meet me in my lostness.

Stuck in stagnancy,
I don't know how to move.
Wandering in circles,
I don't know what I want.

I know You have prepared good works for me, oh Giver,
but they feel obscured by my aimlessness.

The milestones my peers have hit
are but far-off dreams for me.
The goals they meet
strike like hammers to my heart.
Watching my friends race ahead of me,
I feel trapped in a competition I never meant to enter.

Bewildered by those who seem to understand
the invisible rules of how to succeed, I am left in
         the dust—
    in work,
    in relationships,
    in finances,
    in family.

But it is here in the dust, oh Jesus, that You find me.
Show me how my value lies beyond accomplishments.

I have romanticized finding my true calling,
believing my life will have value when I reach it.
Your cross, oh Christ, says otherwise—
I am already valuable enough to die for,
important enough to set free.

There are times I ask, *What do I offer my community?*
But perhaps my question should be, *What can You offer*
         through me?

Lord, may I be content where You have positioned me,
asking for help to see where I'm already brimming with
         blessing.

Replace my thoughts of comparison with compassion,
for I do not know the real stories of the people I envy.

Remind me I have a purpose as unique as Your love
         for me.
Reinvigorate my imagination to dream with You.

What if my current life is preparing me for something I
        can't see?

Oh God, when I feel overlooked and forgotten,
when I ache to be important,
redirect my heart to You who remember me.

Bolster my hope, oh God,
as I leave the competition of comparison
and press onward to You.

Amen.

Psalm 55:22; 139 • John 21:15–22 • 2 Corinthians 10:12 • Galatians 1:10; 2:20 • Philip-pians 2:3

A Blessing for Moving into
a New Neighborhood

How humbling to have a place in this world to call
    home.

Of all the roads,
this street is the one that leads to your front door.
Of all the neighborhoods,
this community is the one where you now live.

Pay attention to the pulse of life already here.

This street is more than a collection of houses and garages,
stoops and yards.
Your neighbors are not incidental.
May Jesus, preeminent in all things,
help you take a wider view of what's happening,
of how your placement is not a coincidence.

153

Consider the history of your neighborhood,
of the lives that came before you.

Like Jacob,
who awakened to the sacredness
of the ground he rested on,
may you look around and say,
Surely the Lord is in this place.

In the mundanity of daily life,
glory can break through.
Signs of resurrection can arise
at this new address.
Look for them.

At the same time, look for those
hidden in the margins of your community.
Discover needs and meet them, as God leads you.

See your neighbors,
and allow yourself to be seen by them.
Do not treat them as projects
but rather as people already loved by God.

May you, also, receive the Lord's care
from those living around you.

May your home be a rest from the cacophony of the city,
the weariness of the suburbs,
the loneliness of the country.

All creation—including this new home—is groaning,
suffering, as we do, from decay and gravity,
from the erosion of fallen time.
Because of this, oh child of God,
stay all the more eager in hope,
all the more aware that this is not your final home.

For now, as you inhabit this neighborhood,
invite others to your table,
grow quick to share your space and time,
and may your warmth and welcome
always point to the truest Light.

Amen.

Genesis 28:16 • Psalm 91:1–2 • Isaiah 1:17; 32:18 • Matthew 5:14; 22:37–40 •
Mark 12:31 • John 13:35 • 1 Corinthians 10:24

For the World

AND HERE YOU ARE—ALIVE. And so much a part of the world. See how it spins and seeks wholeness, just like you and me? Though it groans, it is always reaching for beauty. Let us pursue this glory together, giving one another footholds of hope. Let us be kind to the earth, caring for its well-being the way we care for our own.

As we trace the perimeters of exactly where we are, may we take notice of resurrection. What is dying so that something else may live? What beauty exists for us to explore? Where does the world need healing, and how can we help? Where can we watch, in awe, as miracles appear? For God is at work in the world—may we never forget this—in the way nature renews itself, bodies regenerate, minds expand, and homes become a refuge. We are not lost, and we have not been abandoned. We are being made whole. We are reflections of our perfect Creator who has always been faithful to us. May we step into the world expecting restoration, contributing to it, awakening all that is real and alive among us. God will show us the way. He has already begun.

A Liturgy for Those Who Have Not Seen the World but Want To

Oh God who sees the whole world at once,

You have made an astonishing planet,
filled with colors and creatures,
alive with vistas and vegetation.
Yet I have only seen it from a distance,
glimpsing its glory in photos,
hearing its wonders through stories.

How I long to close the gap
between where I am
and where I wish to be.

How I ache to circle the globe,
to have my own stories to tell.
How I wish to see what You have made
and experience its fullness with You.

How can it be that there are
cultures I have never known,
climates incomparable to my own,
languages I have never understood but want to?

My corner of the world can feel so small,
so limiting, so suffocating.
It feels unfair to cohabitate the earth
and miss the scope of the human experience.

Yet You know my longing as well as my lack.
Perhaps it is enough—for now—
to make my longing known to You;
to dream alongside the One who created
exactly what I yearn to see,
trusting You will bring me where I'm meant to go
at just the right time.

Keep my eyes open to the opportunities
and open doors You will set before me.
Keep my interests inclined to the people and
            places
You will one day take me.

Oh Lord,
the earth is full and beautiful,
and I hope to see more of it.
I cling to the promise that, one day,
when all is made new and redeemed,
I will have eternity to explore.

Until that day, keep my heart steady

so I may be content at home.

And keep my heart wild

so that I remain enchanted with the world.

Amen.

Genesis 1 • Psalm 19:1–2; 31:19 • Ephesians 2:10 • Revelation 21:1–5

A Liturgy for Voting

Oh God who shoulders governments,
who oversees times and seasons,
who raises up rulers and removes them,
giving wisdom to the wise
and knowledge to the discerning—
today is a day of great responsibility.

What a simple act—
to mark a name on a ballot,
to cast a single vote.
Yet the choice is weighty with significance,
deeply affecting cities and nations.

I begin this day by giving thanks:
for the ability to participate in society,
for the opportunity to select presidents and policies,

for the poll workers who volunteer their time
to make sure each vote is properly cast.

I seek an eternal perspective:
to ascribe the appropriate value to this day,
to trust You no matter what,
to place no overwhelming hope or hatred on the outcome.

I ask for wisdom:
to approach the ballot with a renewed mind,
to make a thoughtful and measured decision,
to discern if You are leading me in one way or another,
even if it means voting differently than I have in the past.

Above all, help me live in my community as a person
            of peace,
praying for those whom You sovereignly allow to govern,
for no matter how I view my civic leaders,
You are in control of more than I can ever know.

I trust You and depend upon Your goodness
no matter the results of this day.

Amen.

Isaiah 9:6–7 • Daniel 2:20–22 • Matthew 6:33 • Mark 12:13–17 • Ephesians 5:1–2

A Liturgy for Wartime

Oh God of peace,
You are present even in war.

We begin by calling to mind the face of Christ:
meek and gentle, compassionate and kind,
fully submissive to the Father,
eyes aflame with the intensity of love.

We long for the day when nations no longer
maintain militaries or strategize for battle,
when every tribe and tongue walks in the light of
        the Lord.

Yet as fear tightens its grip around our chests,
as rage burns in our bones,
as injustice shatters our bodies and spirits,
we will be still and know that You are God.

Speak peace to us, even while we are at war.
Speak peace to rulers, even while they plan for attack.
Speak peace to nations, even while the battle rages.
May war be a time when we hunger for Your Spirit more
        than anything else.

Though we may not understand or agree,
there is a time for peace and a time for war.
Thank You that peace is what we long for,
for You, God of peace, have placed this longing in
        our hearts.

While we are at war,
may violence and death come to a swift end,
and may wisdom be a more effective tool than weapons.
May we face our responsibilities without fear,
and be full of courage through Your presence in us.

Though the entire earth quakes,
our souls remain steady in You.
Though nations rise and fall,
we are in awe of the One whose voice melts the earth,
for You have already won the victory we long for.

Comfort Your people, oh God,
and speak tenderly to us
until the time of struggle is over.
Let wisdom be our weapon.
Let stillness be our shield.
We run to You, Strong Tower,
for You are our safe refuge.

In this world we will have trouble,
but we take heart, for You have overcome the world.

Amen.

Psalm 46; 85:8; 126 • Ecclesiastes 3:1, 8 • Isaiah 2:2–5; 40:1–2 • John 16:33 • Romans 16:20 • 2 Corinthians 10:3–4 • Revelation 19:11–16

A Liturgy for Lamenting a Tragedy That Is Far from You

Oh God who is always close,
we long to be present, to give comfort,
to wrap our arms around the broken and hurting.
This tragedy across the globe is so great,
yet it seems there is so little we can do.

You, oh Lord, mourn with those who mourn,
honoring our cries of lament as sacred and purposeful.
Though we are caught up in confusion,
we do not navigate this grief and distance alone.

As we hear of wars and violence,
of children being taken from families,
of families being taken from homes,
of natural disasters and humanitarian crises,
of unbearable griefs that make us retch with agony,
would you teach us how to comfort from afar?

You are the Man of Sorrows and well acquainted with
      grief,
able to sit with the unexplainable,
guiding us through the complexities of pain.
As we share the heaviness of our hearts with You,
would You show us You are grieving as well?

As we shed tears in the places we dwell,
help us to carry, with open hands,
the mystery of Your kindness and goodness.
Help us ask the questions that have no answers,
even while evil persists.

The world is broken,
yet You are the Restorer of all things.
Come close to us now
and even closer to those at the center of disaster.

Though it feels impossible to hope or to help,
may we reach out to one another
and be open-hearted in our pain,
not attempting to explain the unexplainable,
but holding space for lament,
honoring sorrow,
and handling the sacred and fragile with care.

Amen.

Psalm 30; 40:1–4; 126 • Isaiah 40:1–2 • Luke 6:21 • Romans 12:12–15

A Liturgy for Those Overwhelmed by the News

Oh God of all knowledge,
we are overwhelmed.

In the parade of headlines
and consumption of events,
we can feel anxious, angered, and awed,
all within a single blink.
Overstimulated to the point of numbness,
we can forget the good worth working for.

When news stops breaking our heart
and no longer makes us tender,
we know we are consuming it too quickly
and too often.

Turn us from screens to windows,
from paper to people.

May we look at the earth
and not just read about it.

Draw our attention to the miracles not documented
        in print,
the stories not captured in sound bites.

Equip us to be unflinching in labeling evil,
in choosing the side of those who suffer.
Grant us a preference for service over despair.

Teach us, Jesus, how to bear witness
to the pain and beauty of living
amongst other flawed human participants,
just as You did.

Thank You, oh Emmanuel, that You came to save
        the world
and not condemn it,
for we see much to condemn.
The cross is evidence that You can bear more than we can.

Lord, we are overwhelmed,
but You are not.

Amen.

Psalm 112:6–7 • Matthew 11:28–30 • John 3:17 • Romans 12:15 • Philippians 4:6–7

A Blessing for Air Travel

Today as you travel,
may the Lord be your closest companion.

As you dwell between destinations,
may you find surprising stillness
and an unhasty temperament,
buoyed in the fullness of Christ,
to navigate whatever comes.

In crowded terminals,
in overpriced snacks,
in frustrating delays,
accept the mysterious patience offered by the
       Spirit.

171

Look for overwhelmed workers and travelers
and extend the same mercy you have been given.

Filled with trust, you can board your plane.
As you rise on the wings of dawn
and travel to the far side of the sea,
do not fear turbulence,
for even here will God meet you.
You do not travel in a world of chance,
but rather in divine protection,
in a world where the Most High is your safety.

May this flight give you time to reflect
on what's been buried by the rush of routine.
Process what feels undone.
Pray over your life and the lives of others.
Repent with abandon.
Listen for what God may want to say in these suspended
        hours.
As your mind settles,
may your body do the same.

May sunbeams alight through plane windows.
May blue sky and sparkling city lights break through
        clouds.
Let delight fill your heart without cause.
Focus on the Giver of these good things,
and be thankful for the fullness of your life.

Be convinced, up here,
that neither height nor depth,

nor anything else in all of creation,
can separate you from the love of God.

Amen.

Psalm 91:1; 139:7–10 • John 1:16 • Romans 8:38–39 • James 1:17

A Blessing for the Beauty
in the World

Oh God of mysteries and miracles,

How can it be
that with each passing day
You create unique wonders—
handcrafted works of art—
simply for the sake of beauty,
simply for the joy of delight?

How can it be
that You transcend understanding,
yet are seen and known
in daffodils and dewdrops,
in hummingbirds and hibiscus trees,
in the silence of stars on a cold, clear
        night?

In the beginning, You were there.
In the formless and void, You were there.
All that existed was all that You are,
and when You spoke,
life and light began.

We are enchanted, Master and Maker,
by the artistry of the earth.
We are overcome, Author of Existence,
by its eagerness to sing.

As we stand before mountains,
we are comforted,
for You are our rock and our fortress.

As we witness the wildness of storms,
we take heart,
for the wind becomes still at the sound of Your voice.

As we marvel at sunsets,
our souls are set free,
for the One who paints the sky has a purpose for our lives.

As we gaze upon full moons,
we are humbled by grandeur,
for galaxies and gravity exist within Your domain.

As we witness the first blossoms after winter,
we are filled with hope,
for You have created a world bound for resurrection.

Your voice is all around us,
speaking through the things that live.
The mountains and rocks compose melodies,
the trees of the field clap their hands,
for even creation worships You.

Thank You for revealing Yourself
through these small wonders.
Open our eyes even more to these daily miracles
so that we may join them in their song.

Amen.

Genesis 1 • Psalm 16:9–11; 19:1; 105 • Isaiah 55:12 • John 1:1–5

Acknowledgments

To Chris Park, what a gift to be on the same team. We can't imagine where we'd be without your nurturing guidance, brilliant straight-shooting, advocacy, and reminders of who we write for in the first place.

To our editors—Becky Nesbitt and Leita Williams—thank you for taking such good care of our words with your fresh insights and enthusiastic feedback. It was easy to trust our vision with you two. Many thanks also to the entire WaterBrook team: Julia Wallace, Liza Stepanovich, Abby Duval, Mark Maguire, Sarah Horgan, Jessie Bright, Daniel Christensen, Hannah Frank, Elizabeth Eno, Brett Benson, Douglas Mann, and many more who have helped make this book as beautiful as it could be.

To our Women of Words, thank you for every chapter and volume. To be known and loved by each of you is a gift. Sarah Jane, your tender bravery inspires us to pursue truth without compromising honesty. Charissa, your wisdom and freedom inspire us to be our whole selves without shame. Maddie, your leadership and steadfastness keep us anchored to the Spirit. Corinne, your buoyancy and fierce loyalty create a home for us. Kristalyn, your intentionality and passion draw out richer versions of ourselves, inspiring us to become the women we always wished we could be. Serena, your discernment and adventurous spirit bring constant refreshment and nourishment to our souls. Thank you—all of you. Let's keep pursuing beauty together.

To Kiana and Alexa, thank you for Praise Mondays, Confession Wednesdays, and Affirmation Fridays, for the countless voice-memo prayers and the years' worth of trust that has been built as a core group. We would not be the women we are today without both of you.

I (Audrey) am grateful first to my parents: Mark and Leslie Elledge, who have never flinched in the face of my writing pursuits. Your names always rise to the top of my gratitude list. And thank you to Carlos, whose unwavering encouragement, humor, and presence both buoy and bolster me.

Thanks also to my entire family, all of whom have gone out of their way to share my writing with others, attend book events, and privately encourage me.

Lastly, thank you to my community, whose prayers anchored me amid writer's block, deadlines, and more. Thank you to my sweet church family, Peace in the City; my kind roommate, Kenya Bell, who let me turn our apartment into a writing lair; and my friends and soulmates—you know who you are.

I (Elizabeth) want to thank Matthew, Haven, David, Michael, Annie, Hudson, Owen, John David, Alli, Lily, and Levi for bringing so much joy to my life and for continuously supporting me no matter what. Thank you also to my mom and dad for cheering me on, for being my safe place, for loving exactly who I am, and for providing a space where tears and laughter can be shared in abundance.

Thank you to our Church of the City New York family for faithfully pursuing presence, formation, and mission together. We long to see God bring His love and peace to New York as it is in heaven.

Finally, our greatest thanks and awe to the Word, our dearest confidant and friend, and the Spirit, who interceded with the words we did not have.

About the Authors

AUDREY ELLEDGE is an author and editor in New York, where she works by day at SparkNotes. She has won the Academy of American Poets Prize and the Virginia Beall Ball Prize. Audrey co-authored her first book, *Liturgies for Hope,* with Elizabeth Moore.

ELIZABETH MOORE lives in New York, where she works for Ad Age and attends Church of the City New York. She co-authored her first book, *Liturgies for Hope,* with Audrey Elledge.

About the Type

This book was set in Baskerville, a typeface designed by John Baskerville (1706–75), an amateur printer and typefounder, and cut for him by John Handy in 1750. The type became popular again when the Lanston Monotype Corporation of London revived the classic roman face in 1923. The Mergenthaler Linotype Company in England and the United States cut a version of Baskerville in 1931, making it one of the most widely used typefaces today.